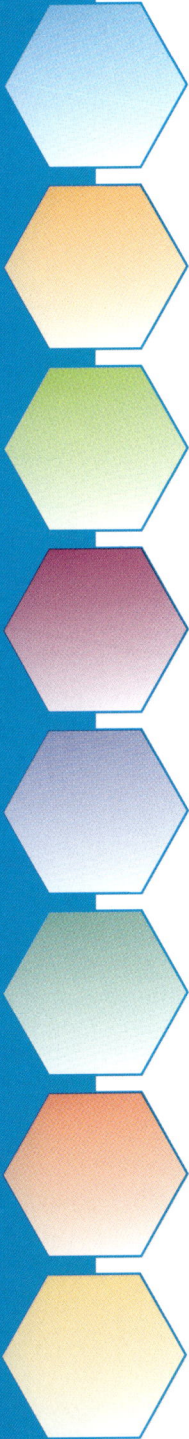

Learning

to

Learn

Accountancy

First edition 2002
Second edition October 2007

ISBN 9780 7517 4179 7
(Previous ISBN 0 7517 1063 6)

British Library Cataloguing-in-Publication Data
A catalogue record for this book is available from the British Library

Published by

BPP Learning Media Ltd
Aldine House, Aldine Place
London W12 8AW

www.bpp.com

Printed in Great Britain by

Ashford Colour Press
Unit 600
Fareham Reach
Fareham Road
Gosport
Hants PO13 0FW

Contents

Learning
styles

Types of
subject

Study
environment

Study
skills

Revision

Types of
question

Exam
paper

An
assortment

Preface

Preface

Learning accountancy

You've committed yourself to passing your accountancy exams. However you may not be completely clear yet about what you'll be studying. You've studied before of course, at school certainly, at university perhaps. You know studying accountancy will be a bit different, but how different?

Knowledge and skills

Accountancy exams will give you the knowledge and skills you need to occupy a senior position in the workplace.

Accountancy qualifications are designed to be broad-based, giving you the opportunity to work in a variety of different environments. To qualify, you thus need knowledge of a variety of subjects.

Accountancy exams also test ways in which you use your knowledge. This means applying what you know to solving problems and communicating your solutions clearly. The exams aim to mimic the complexities of real life and they demand that you think carefully about how to approach different situations.

Time

One other concern you may have is the time available for study. The first exams may be six months rather than two years away. You have more commitments now than you ever had before.

The description we've given of studying for accountancy exams may have raised a number of questions in your mind.

Well that's a start. One thing we want you to do throughout your studies is to think constantly about *how* you're learning and *what* you're learning.

What we've done on the next couple of pages is ask a BPP author some questions about how she learned accountancy. We suggest that you try to answer the questions in relation to exams that you've previously taken.

► If you struggle with any of the questions, *don't worry*; this book will give you the answers.

► If you don't understand why the questions are significant, *don't worry*; this book will explain their importance.

► If you feel that the questions have highlighted weaknesses in what you've done before, *don't worry*; this book will help you eliminate those weaknesses.

In this book we're going to show you how you can learn accountancy

► **Efficiently** We don't want you to spend unnecessary time studying.

► **Effectively** We do want you to pass your exams.

> "Exams are credentials, qualifications, the footlings of your CV, your cheat's visa."

Alan Bennett, *The History Boys*

Questions

Q1 How did accountancy exams differ from previous exams you's taken?

Having read History at university, it was a bit of a shock to get back to studying a lot of different subjects, and encountering types of questions that I hadn't seen in exams before. Also in accountancy exams you're given a lot of information in questions that you have to use selectively in your answers and you have to think very carefully about the techniques you use.

Q2 Did you know about learning styles, or have any idea what your strengths/weaknesses were in this area?

I didn't know anything about different intelligences etc. However, I was aware that I was a more 'wordy' than 'numbery' person, if you know what I mean.

Q3 So, had you studied any of the subjects you faced in your accountancy exams before?

Not at all. I thought about doing Economics A level, but chose Latin instead. That was really helpful when it came to accountancy, you can imagine! Well, except on some of the law papers. It was all really new to me. Some of it felt like a different language.

Q4 Did you find you had any subject preferences?

Unsurprisingly I suppose, given what I've said about being wordy, I showed a clear preference in my first year for law and management. But I also surprised myself by finding economics interesting - I'd thought that I'd find it really hard.

Q5 What study method did you use?

My firm chose the 'link' method for me, which meant that I attended training college for a series of single weeks.

Q6 When did you study privately?

In my first year, it seemed like all the time! All the subjects were new, and I found that it took me a long time to understand everything. As I got more familiar with the subjects, I found I could use my time more effectively. I tended to work in the evenings and early mornings round my lectures. When not at college I found it easier to study early before I went to work than trying to do it after a whole day at work - but that is just me, I'm a morning person.

Q7 Where did you study?

In the course of three years, lots of places. In my first year I worked in my bedroom while living in someone else's house. In my second year, I got my own place and worked in the living room. I often went into college early to run through my notes and do question practice. I sometimes worked in the office in the mornings or the library. I did a lot of revision on the bus as well.

Q8 Did you plan your own work?

Yes, within the boundaries of the homework given to me by my tutors. I used to set up general plans for the weeks between attending college and I particularly used to plan revision, before I went on the revision course at the college. That way I knew that I had reviewed things I found difficult before it was revised in class.

Q9 How much study did you used to do?

It really depended on circumstances. Between visits to college I used to try and work on the principle of doing an hour in the morning where possible, and perhaps an hour plus in the evening at minimum. If I missed one day, I'd try to catch up on another. Sometimes however there were weeks where I was working overtime or travelling a long way, and it wasn't really viable to study before and after, so I didn't. And once in a while it was good to consciously take a break. I always tried to keep at least one day at the weekend 'study free', but it wasn't always possible, especially close to the exams.

Q10 How did you find lectures?

It soon became apparent that I am not a very aural learner. I found it difficult to concentrate on what was said, and found that I had to take notes of what the lecturer was saying to focus on it. Once I had got to grips with listening, it was good to be talked through things in a simple, clear way.

Q11 What was your favourite 'study skill'?

Notetaking. I made copious notes (on lectures, textbooks, questions ...). I found that the act of writing stuff helped me to remember it, and trying to put it into my own words helped me to understand it better.

Q12 Do you have a favourite revision tip?

I have two favourite techniques - posters and index cards (now, of course, I write passcards for other people!). Index cards have seen me through Uni and accountancy now. I think I must have an A5 shaped brain! But just because I like them doesn't mean everyone else will. Revision is a very individual thing.

Q13 What sort of time scale did you set on revising?

I tried to make sure that I had a handle on everything before I went on my revision course, so that it genuinely was revision. Sometimes that meant revising things from early in the teaching course just before revision started. Generally though I set myself up a revision timetable from day one of the revision course - dovetailing with my tutor's recommendations when it was right for me.

Q14 Did you do question practice?

Yes. Basically I am a swot and I mainly do what people tell me to do! Particularly on the 'numbery' papers, especially financial accounting, I found that it was the only way to get my approach right and eliminate silly errors. I have to admit on 'wordy' papers I sometimes restricted myself to an answer plan, because I was fairly convinced that my essay style was okay.

Q15 Did you get things marked?

Yes. Course exams and mocks were always marked.

Q16 How did you approach exam day?

Unfortunately I am dreadful at exams. I get unfeasibly nervous about going into exam halls. So you would have found me outside, taking really deep breaths and trying not to be sick, trying to relax. Not the best start! Once I got in there, I knew I had to concentrate on exam technique so I was really strict about timings on questions. Practising in exam conditions is a real help for that.

How this book can help you

How you study

We shall show you how to understand and remember the material you learn. We shall challenge you to assess where your strengths lie, and also how to find out where you need to do most work.

We shall also discuss organising your studies, particularly during the critical period in the run up to the exams. And as for the exams - we'll show you how to approach those as well.

Where and when you study

We shall be looking at the environment in which you study; studying in the right place with the right atmosphere can enhance the effectiveness and efficiency of your study. As you have limited time, we shall also discuss when to study and how much to do.

What you study

We shall provide a brief introduction to the most important subjects that you will meet. We also cover the key skills you need to pass - most importantly how to approach the different types of question that you will encounter.

We suggest • • •

that you read this book from cover to cover first of all to see what it can offer you. Then throughout your studies you can dip in and out of it depending on what assistance you need at any one time.

Learning
styles

Types of
subject

Study
environment

Study
skills

Revision

Types of
question

Exam
paper

An
assortment

Learning
styles

Introduction

This book aims to help you to be proactive in your accountancy studies. It is not about learning accountancy. It is about learning to learn accountancy.

Learning is often something that people fear, particularly if it is something they have chosen to study while trying to carry out a full-time job as well.

In this Chapter, we will explore some features of learning that you may not have considered before. There are a number of different methods of learning; we shall investigate which suits you best. Then in further chapters we shall focus on different methods of

▶ Obtaining knowledge
▶ Answering questions
▶ Facing exams

We shall try and look at the best way for YOU to do each of these things, based on what we discover in this Chapter about how YOU learn best.

Let's have a look at two definitions which will be important to use in the course of understanding this book.

To obtain knowledge of facts or of how to do things, or an understanding of ideas.

Learn

To give knowledge

Teach

There is a difference between being taught and learning. Being taught is a passive thing, and we want it to be a proactive thing, and we want you to be proactive in your studies.

It is in the nature of a gift that you do not have to (or may feel unable to) accept something that is given to you.

This book aims to help you to make the effective link between the gift, and acceptance of the knowledge.

You may find that you agree with Festus, who said in c59 AD:

" . . . much learning doth make thee mad. "

We hope that after reading this book, you'll have **changed your mind**.

Lectures

Accountancy is commonly taught aurally, that is, in lecture theatres at professional training centres or colleges.

You may be booked onto a course at a BPP centre, either to study for an extended period on release from work, or intermittently or in the evenings.

Lectures are a very effective way for people who have knowledge to give that knowledge to a group of people at the same time. For your employers, it is also an economically sound method: to engage individual tutors for each of you would probably be cost-prohibitive.

However, most people have an experience similar to 'the Martian experience' (outlined to the left) in their studies, some have them more than others. A key part of turning teaching into learning will be to identify how you respond to lectures, and putting plans into action to convert the teaching you receive into learning.

Have you ever sat in a lecture, and found that the lecturer's voice is very soporific, the room seems to be getting warmer, and your mind wanders to any and every subject under the sun except the task in hand and the content of the lecture?

The lecturer is talking with more and more emphasis, and waving her hands around a little, scribbling earnestly on the overhead projector screen. It is clear that this is the most important part of the lecture to this point, but all you can picture is what Mars might look like. The classroom is beginning to feel weightless, and all your classmates are beginning to look a little green...

"Such labour'd nothings, in so strange a style, amaze th' unlearned, and make the learned smile."

Alexander Pope

IDENTIFY how you respond to lectures

DEVELOP action plans

IMPLEMENT the plans & start **LEARNING**

Converting teaching • • •

'...and you should consolidate these accounts...'

'...what have I got for dinner...'

Home study

Another common way of studying for accountancy is to undertake a course of Home Study. You may be enrolled on a BPP Home Study PLUS course.

Of course, even if you are not enrolled on such a course, taking any kind of accountancy training will involve you studying some part of your course at home in the form of homework from lectures, or your own development of what you have been taught - your own personal learning.

A BPP Study Text in some ways acts a personal trainer. The author is giving you knowledge through the pages. If you are on a BPP Home Study PLUS programme, you are also offered a tailored study plan of how to approach the textbook and practice questions, and on-line support.

Studying on your own can lead to those dramatic, head-exploding moments (outlined to the right) from time to time. In order to learn accountancy effectively by this method you need also to identify how you approach such learning and then put an effective study system into place, using all the elements made available to you.

...Alternatively this may be your experience...

You've been in the library for two hours. You have your BPP Study Text open before you, and have read page 12 three times. You could now recite the titles, authors and publishers of the row of books in front of you in the correct order and win millions on a quiz show, but couldn't tell anyone how to fill in their personal tax return for love nor money.

The skin on your head is feeling a bit tight. As the seconds tick by, you can feel it getting tighter and tighter, until your head explodes. Here endeth the problem...

"Books cannot always please, however good. Minds are not always craving for their food."

George Crabbey

• • • into learning!

Learning styles questionnaire

Over the following few pages, we shall be trying to assess what types of intelligence you exhibit more strongly and prefer to use. There are two illustrations for you to work through.

Learning styles identification, Illustration 1

Please work through the following questionnaire and tick the boxes **where you agree with the statement.**

Do not think too hard about your answers. This questionnaire consists of 70 questions, but should take you no more than about 5 minutes to answer.

Learning styles questionnaire guidance

Do you agree with the statement? Answering yes or no . . .

If your answer is	ALWAYS	Answer 'yes'	$\Rightarrow$	tick the box
If your answer is	USUALLY	Answer 'yes'	$\Rightarrow$	tick the box
If your answer is	SOMETIMES	Answer 'yes'	$\Rightarrow$	tick the box
If your answer is	SOMETIMES (rarely)	Answer 'no'	$\Rightarrow$	do nothing
If your answer is	NEVER	Answer 'no'	$\Rightarrow$	do nothing

Please work through the illustrations **honestly**.

If you do not, the study systems we guide you towards later in the book will not necessarily be effective for you.

But **don't think too hard** about this questionnaire – give us your **gut answer**.

Questionnaire

1 I love words ☑

2 I love rhythm ☐

3 I picture things ☑

4 I am 'a doer' ☑

5 I like to follow a 'step approach' to complete a task ☑

6 I think actions speak louder than words ☑

7 I find it easy to explain things to other people ☐

8 I like to mull things over in my head ☑

9 I make lists ☑

10 I like to take a moment to order my thoughts ☐

11 My doodles are predominately made of words ☐

12 I am good with my hands ☐

13 I find myself singing advert jingles ☑

14 My doodles are predominately made of pictures or symbols ☑

15 I love chess (the game) ☐

16 I discuss something with others to work out what it means ☑

17 I like to work something out for myself ☐

18 I always go for logic puzzles ☐

19 I will more easily understand how to do something if I do it ☑

20 I like riddles ☑

21 If I was going grocery shopping I would make a list ☑

22 If I was going grocery shopping I would visualise me, or someone else, cooking, and the ingredients they would need ☑

23 If I was going grocery shopping I would tell someone what I wanted to buy and take that person with me ☐

24 If I was going grocery shopping I would organise my shopping list so it correlated to the shop layout ☐

25 When someone sings a nursery rhyme I see the characters in my head ☐

26 I could hum three nursery rhymes if you asked me to ☐

27 I choose birthday cards primarily because of the message in the words ☐

28 I choose birthday cards primarily because of the picture on the front ☐

29 I would like to send a gorilla-gram in place of a card ☐

30 If I was planning a ski trip I would read a book about skiing ☐

31 I think that I would enjoy skiing ☐

32 If I was planning a ski trip I would look at maps and pictures of the pistes ☐

33 If I was planning a ski trip I would talk to someone who can ski ☐

34 If I was planning a ski trip I would visit a snow-dome ☐

35 I think that I would probably hate skiing ☐

36 If I was planning a ski trip I would starting hearing the Ski Sunday music in my head ☐

37 I like big groups of people ☐

38 I can spend hours talking on the phone ☐

39 I like to meet my friends in groups ☐

40 I like to see my friends on a one-to-one basis, or in smaller groups ☐

41 I have strong opinions ☐

42 People value my opinions and tell me so ☐

43 If I want to remember things I write them down ☐

44 If I want to remember things I repeat them to myself over and over again ☐

45 If I want to remember things I set them to tunes in my head ☐

46 If I want to remember things I attach numbers to them to make it easier ☐

47 I recall things by counting them off on my fingers ☐

48 If I want to remember things I picture them ☐

49 I stay behind after lectures and ask questions if I don't understand ☐

50 I ask questions in class ☐

51 I like to ask the next day when I have had time to think about it ☐

52 If writing an essay, I find it easy to put my thoughts in order ☐

53 I like to draw up an essay plan ☐

54 I prefer to be given a diagram than a page of text ☐

55 I can always calculate the score gained in darts easily ☐

56	I have a favourite song	☐
57	I use my hands a lot when I speak	☐
58	I would like a small wedding with close friends and family attending	☐
59	I enjoy team games	☐
60	I enjoy 'Pictionary'	☐
61	I play a musical instrument, or the spoons, pots and pans, or anything...	☐
62	I am the navigator in the family	☐
63	If I was having a dinner-party, I would like to draw up a seating plan	☐
64	I would like to try rock climbing	☐
65	I am good at 'Name that tune'	☐
66	People notice that I am well co-ordinated	☐
67	I enjoy word games such as 'Taboo' and 'Articulate'	☐
68	I am a champion 'Twister' player	☐
69	I always take charge of tuning the radio in	☐
70	I prefer a game like Solitare to a group game	☐

Before you turn to find the 'answers' of this questionnaire, please take time to work through illustration 2 (on the next page).

This is probably a good time to note, however, that there are no right answers to this questionnaire.

It is an observation of how you think, not a test.

Therefore when you do turn to the answers, the number of boxes you tick off does not matter. The 'answer' will lie in the ratio of answers you have given, not the absolute answers.

Therefore ● ● ●

DO NOT cast your eye back over this questionnaire and think - 'I haven't answered very many' or 'I've answered too many' and be tempted to amend your answers.

The number of statements identified with is irrelevant. Honestly - there are no high or low scores. You will use your answers only to compare with your own answers.

Learning styles identification, Illustration 2

In the blank page given above please put down all your thoughts about Elephants.

Again: Do not think too hard about this task.
Just do it!

You can take as long as you like over this task.

The seven intelligences

If asked to describe intelligence, you might have referred to really clever people, people who like books, who did a Phd at University, or something along those lines.

Or you may already be aware of the fact that it is now generally accepted that people have a variety of intelligences, or ways in which they learn. Traditionally learning through our linguistic intelligence has been focused on, now there are seven different areas to focus learning in.

You might think that this is terrifying:

"Seven ways of learning! I find the one I've got difficult enough…"

But as we shall see in the following pages, this is good news. Learning can be tailored to the way you think - not the other way around.

The boxes on the right are going to summarise the results of your questionnaire (illustration 1).

Total

Linguistic

| 1 | 9 | 11 | 20 | 21 | 27 | 30 | 38 | 43 | 67 |

Maths logical

| 5 | 15 | 18 | 24 | 46 | 47 | 52 | 53 | 55 | 63 |

Spatial visual

| 3 | 14 | 22 | 25 | 28 | 32 | 48 | 54 | 60 | 62 |

Musical

| 2 | 13 | 26 | 29 | 36 | 45 | 56 | 61 | 65 | 69 |

Bodily kinaesthetic

| 4 | 6 | 12 | 19 | 31 | 34 | 57 | 64 | 66 | 68 |

Interpersonal

| 7 | 16 | 23 | 33 | 37 | 39 | 42 | 49 | 50 | 59 |

Intra-personal

| 8 | 10 | 17 | 35 | 40 | 41 | 44 | 51 | 58 | 70 |

Analysing the results, Illustration 1

Tick the boxes above that are attached to the numbers of the statements you agreed with in the questionnaire. They are jumbled here because they are grouped by the intelligence that they indicate. We'll discuss the intelligences over the following pages. You are likely to have some ticks in most areas, but a higher number of ticks in two or three. However, there is no wrong answer - everyone is different. You may find that you prefer to learn in one way, or a large variety of ways…

Interpersonal

Interpersonal people are those people who find it natural to interact heavily with other people in the thought and learning process.

They will regularly question a person who is teaching them, they will discuss what they have learned with other people, they will seek to understand things through conversing through them, they will be happy to summarise what they have learned for other people.

These people are likely to be natural teachers or salespeople, communicating with others comes naturally to them. They may find they do the following:

▶ Interact with groups of other people without concern

▶ Bounce ideas off other people

▶ Talk things through with people if they are worried about something

▶ Brainstorm corporately (with others)

People tend to fall into one or other of the personal categories, which stand slightly apart from the other five categories. It is likely that you scored higher in one of these two categories than the other and unlikely you scored nothing in either category.

If you want to develop your interpersonal intelligence, try the following:

▶ Ring your mum after lectures and explain all the concepts you have learned in the day

▶ Pick three items of news out of the newspaper every day and discuss them with someone else.

▶ Join a debating club

▶ Volunteer to help out at a children's club or school

Interpersonal people

" Liz is a **people person.** "

" Frank always knows the right thing to say. I always go to him if I'm down or want advice. "

Intrapersonal

Intrapersonal people are people who think things through themselves before discussing them with others. They are likely to be self-aware and good managers of themselves.

They may find that communicating with others does not come naturally to them. This does not mean that they are not good at it when they do communicate with others.

An intrapersonal person might do the following:

▶ Keep their thoughts to themselves

▶ Reflect on issues before coming to a conclusion

▶ Often seek time alone to think

▶ Brainstorm privately

To develop your skills, you could try the following:

▶ Pick three topics out of the newspaper every day, and consciously spend ten minutes thinking through the issues you see being raised.

▶ When you want to ask a question, stop. Note the question down, but allow yourself some time to think through the question raised and see if you can come up with the answer yourself.

These 'personal' intelligences will have strong links with your other key intelligences, which you will see as you read through the following pages.

For example, a linguistic interpersonal person may communicate in words, a spatial visual intrapersonal person may think things through in pictures.

Intrapersonal people

"Amir is a reflective person - **he always gives a well thought out answer.**"

"Susan is a think-tank. She'll sort through an idea for you."

Linguistic

When I have worked through illustrations such as the questionnaire you completed earlier in this Chapter, I have found that I come out as highly linguistic.

This makes sense to me. I love words, enjoy observing correlation and links between different languages, am a writer, enjoy games such as 'Articulate'.

This may also be true for you. If it is not, however, you may want to develop your linguistic intelligence by trying some of the following things:

▶ *Reading magazines/books on subjects which interest you*

▶ *Challenging yourself to learn ten new words a week*

▶ *Telling your teddy two minutes worth of interesting information every morning.*

Linguistic people are those people who are comfortable with and enjoy language, or words.

Not every linguistic person will enjoy all the same things, but here's a list of things which a linguistic person might find interesting, relate to or enjoy:

▶ Word games
▶ Reading
▶ Making speeches
▶ Poetry
▶ Learning other languages
▶ Grammar
▶ Crosswords
▶ Thesauruses

Being linguistic does not mean you will be very good at writing - you may never have learned to write - but that you enjoy words. This can reveal itself in the fact that you love to talk, or read, that is, any activity that involves words as opposed to pictures.

A^{nt} B^{ag} C_{rystallisation}

Linguistic people

"Betty's really got the **gift of the gab.**"

"Jason's a total bookworm. He's always got his head stuck in a book."

Mathematical logical

Mathematical logical people are people who are comfortable with and enjoy numbers, and a system of thought which follows a certain reason. Such people are often analysts, and very rational.

Accountants are commonly mathematical logical people, so don't be surprised if you fall into this category. However, also don't be alarmed if you do not: accountants call on a great variety of skills, that is part of the challenge of studying to become an accountant.

Here is a list of activities or thoughts that a mathematical logical person may enjoy or relate to:

▶ Su Doku
▶ Rubic cube
▶ Logic puzzles
▶ 'Cluedo'
▶ Prioritisation
▶ Patterns

Mathematical logical people can help you if you are on a budget in the supermarket and you've forgotten your calculator, because they are usually quick with numbers and can do mental arithmetic.

They are also useful if you want to remember a phone number or a date.

Mathematical logical people are the people who, when they watch thrillers or detective films, can work out 'whodunnit' before the ending is revealed. If you are not one, you must know one...always one step ahead of Poirot, analysing, considering, never suspending their disbelief...

If you want to develop your mathematical logical intelligence, try one or more of the following activities:

▶ *Become a scorer for a darts or cricket team*

▶ *Challenge yourself to grocery shop to a budget without a calculator*

▶ *Get someone to quiz you in mental arithmetic over breakfast.*

Mathematical logical people

"Pawandeep has always had a **head for figures.**"

"Rick's as sharp as a knife. One day he'll cut himself"

Spatial visual

The spatial side of spatial visual may be a little bit difficult to understand.

It is people who seem to be at one with their environment, seem never to get lost - so are good natural navigators. They notice things around them, so that they can identify where they are in relation to their surroundings.

They can also judge space by sight, so for example, as stated below, they would be able to judge easily whether their car would fit into a parking space by looking at it.

If you want to develop your spatial visual intelligence, try some of the following:

▶ *Go somewhere you don't know as a passenger (by car or bus) and focus on noticing your environment. Then try to navigate back again.*

▶ *Try some simple drawing or diagramming.*

Spatial visual people are those people who are comfortable with or enjoy their spatial environment (the things that are around them) and visual things such as pictures and art.

Again, this does not mean that they are necessarily great artists. It means that they prefer pictures to words. It means that if someone is telling them about something, they can picture the scene, or if they do read books, they can strongly visualise the characters and scenes as they unfold.

As always, not everyone who displays spatial visual tendencies will enjoy the same things, but here's a list of activities and concepts that a spatial visual person might enjoy or relate to:

▶ Drawing
▶ Cartoons
▶ Films
▶ Treasure hunts
▶ Orienteering
▶ Mindmaps

Spatial visual people

“Katie's got an amazing **sense of direction.**”

“Phil always parks the car - he can always tell whether the car will fit in the space.”

Musical

Musical people are those people who are comfortable with, and enjoy, music, rhyme and/or rhythm.

Again, a person who falls into the musical category may not find that they like or are comfortable with all these things, but rather one or two, or a selection. There may be a strong overlap between a linguistic person who enjoys poetry for the words and also the musical side of poetry in the metre and rhyme. Alternatively, a musical person might not appreciate rhyme, but have perfect pitch or be able to play any musical instrument available.

Here is a list of activities that a musical person may enjoy:

▶ Attending concerts
▶ Listening to a walkman or radio
▶ Creating limericks
▶ Playing a musical instrument
▶ Humming/whistling/singing in the shower
▶ Dancing

Musical people

" Ella's just got **rhythm, man** "

" John's always humming or whistling - always got a tune. "

Bodily kinaesthetic

Bodily kinaesthetic people are people who are comfortable with, and enjoy, doing things and being active. They are most likely to learn how to do something if they are shown how to do it, and then do it for themselves.

This is likely to mean that they are 'trial and error' people, that is, people who don't mind making mistakes the first time, because if they keep doing something they will get it right in the end. They understood the theory they were told in school that 'practice makes perfect'.

Here is a list of activities or thoughts that a bodily kinaesthetic person may enjoy or relate to:

▶ Sport
▶ Craft
▶ Design and technology
▶ 'Hands on' experience
▶ Good hand-eye co-ordination
▶ Games like 'Jenga' and 'Pick up stix'

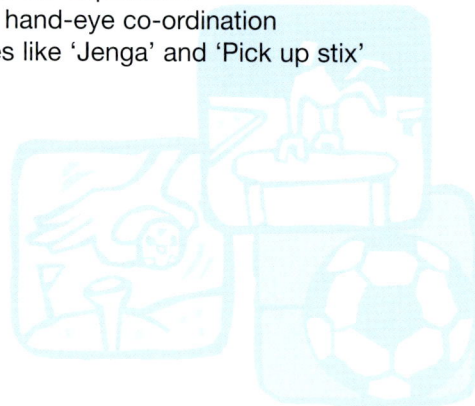

Bodily kinaesthetic people

"Peter is really good with **his hands.**"

"Mai's got amazing hand-eye co-ordination."

Analysing the elephant

Having read about the different types of intelligence that we possess, look back at what you produced in illustration 2.

Does what you produced reflect the results of your questionnaire?

For example, a person who strongly portrays linguistic intelligence will have used words to describe an elephant, a visual person may have doodled bits of elephant, for example, tusks, big ears, trunk.

A maths-logical person may have approached the issue by recognising groups of ideas, for example by using headings such as habitat, appearance etc...

A musical person may have written a rhyme, or thought immediately of the song 'Nellie the Elephant'.

A bodily kinaesthetic person may have written nothing or lots down, but not before they instinctively raised their arm to their face like a trunk (or wanted to!).

Elephants

Elephants are mammals found particularly in Africa and the Indian subcontinent.

They are characterised by their large trunks and their distinctive tusks which have long been the target of poachers...

The elephant is seen as being a very wise animal, hence the saying that 'an elephant never forgets...'

Ivory ➝ Poachers

Tusks   Africa   Memory

ELEPHANTS

Mammal

Habitat	Features	Other aspects
Africa	Tusk	Ivory
Indian sub-continent	Trunk	Poaching
Trees	Big ears	Memory
Plains	Molars	

An elephant is big and grey
And in the mud he likes to play
He never will forget a thing
And his great trunk he likes to swing
He pushes down trees to eat their bark
Hence he leaves his special mark
I like the African best I fear,
Because I like his great big ears

Nellie the elephant packed her trunk, and said goodbye to the circus ...

The results of the elephant illustration

This is not a sure-fire illustration, because we have all been taught to respond in a certain way. Although the illustration did not tell you to write, **you made an assumption** that you were **to use words**, because that is how you usually answer questions.

However, think back to your initial responses to the instruction and see if they fit with the intelligence brackets which you have identified yourself with.

Further analysis

Here is a series of questions for you to think about. This time, instead of just giving your gut answer, think about why you have given that answer and what it shows about the type of intelligence you prefer to use.

Some pointers are given to help you think these through.

Q Are you the sort of person who will observe, 'I hate to watch a film when I've read the book'?

Did you answer

Yes?

... because I hate to watch DVDs — Does this indicate you are not very **visual?**

...because the film spoils the pictures in my head — Are you **visual?**

No?

...because I never read books — Does this indicate you are not **linguistic?**

...because I am indifferent to this sentence — Are you neither **visual** or **linguistic?**

Q If I was to tell you that the next thing that I am going to tell you will be true, but the last thing I told you was a lie, would you believe me?

Did you answer

Yes?

... because I see no reason to disbelieve you — Does this indicate you have not noticed the flawed **logic** in this sentence?

No?

...because the sentence cannot be true — Still not quite getting the **logic. . .**

Nothing?

...because you know the sentence is not logical — Are you **logical?**

Did you think it through or go away and talk it through with a group of friends? (Are you intrapersonal or interpersonal?)

Think about it!

Next time someone else says something along these lines, spend a moment wondering why they are saying it. Perhaps you might even ask them what their reasoning was. It is probably because they are showing an **intellectual preference**. Only some of the intelligences have been illustrated here. There are endless examples:

A **musical** person might be annoyed by inaccurate tuning on a radio that you have not even noticed...
A **bodily kinaesthetic** person may be irritated by an activity that requires them to sit still...
Someone who is **intrapersonal** might find a fast-paced lecture with no breaks difficult - they haven't had a chance to think...

Visual, aural or practical?

Before we leave this chapter, it doesn't hurt to explore your preferences between visual, aural or practical learning. There are some obvious links between these concepts and the intelligences we have just outlined (these are indicated in the right hand column) but the links do not have to, and may not, be obvious in your case.

Try the following questions, noting your preferences in terms of most preferred (1) to least preferred (3), with (2) being the one in the middle.

A   When I am learning something, I would rather:

Hear it	☐	**A**
Read it	☐	**V**
Do it myself	☐	**P**

B   In leisure time I like to:

Go to the cinema	☐	**V**
Do something active	☐	**P**
Go to a concert	☐	**A**

C   I would be annoyed by:

Colour clashes	☐	**V**
Dissonance	☐	**A**
Physical restraint	☐	**P**

D   I am indifferent to:

Work experience	☐	**P**
Lectures	☐	**A**
Libraries	☐	**V**

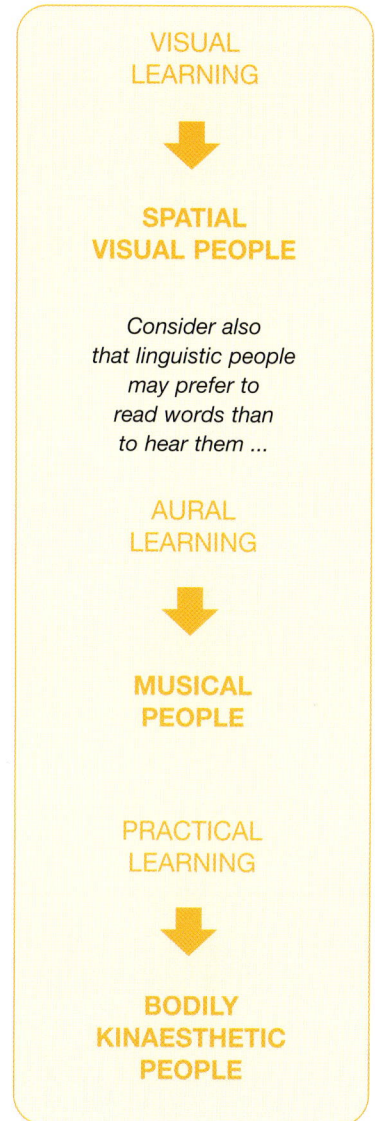

VISUAL LEARNING

⬇

SPATIAL VISUAL PEOPLE

Consider also that linguistic people may prefer to read words than to hear them ...

AURAL LEARNING

⬇

MUSICAL PEOPLE

PRACTICAL LEARNING

⬇

BODILY KINAESTHETIC PEOPLE

E   I am irritated by:

Changes in light quality	☐	**V**
Changes in temperature	☐	**P**
Persistent, unintentional noises	☐	**A**

F   When trying to concentrate I would notice:

Sirens	☐	**A**
Flashing lights	☐	**V**
Whether I am still or not	☐	**P**

G   If I was teaching someone else something, I would:

Show them	☐	**P**
Tell them	☐	**A**
Email them	☐	**V**

Analysing this questionnaire

Look back over the last two pages and tot up your total scores for 'P', 'V' and 'A' statements. If you have one which is lower than the others, you are likely to have a clear preference for how you receive information, if you have similar scores for each, you appear to be indifferent between methods of receiving information.

Lastly, cast your mind back over the ways you have been given information in the past and what your experiences of that have been, just to check this indication is correct. If this suggests you are highly aural, yet you hated lectures at University, have you been totally honest in your answers? Of course, you may just have been subjected to some poor lectures ...

And finally ...

One last observation about learning styles

Broadly speaking, people carry two attitudes into studying.

These are summarised to the right.

Which do you feel you most identify with?

Neither of the positions is right or wrong. However, as with all the things we have discussed so far, it is best to identify what your prevailing attitude is, so that you can incorporate that understanding into your approach to your study and study materials.

Some people like to think practically. They are prepared to learn theory, but only after they can clearly see why it is needed in practice, and how the theory will be put to use. This is what we are going to refer to as the 'WHY?' position.

Some people like theory. They prefer to get to grips with what the theory is before they start thinking about how to put it into practice. This is what we are going to refer to as the 'WHAT?' position.

Why?

If you are the kind of person that feels that they will not be able to come to terms with a theory unless they have been given a chance to **'see it in action'** or at least understand where the theory will be **relevant in practice**, you may find the idea of opening a text book and wading through theory very off-putting.

There is a solution which you might consider. When approaching study materials, flick through looking for case examples or questions. Reading through these should **indicate the practicalities of a theory** before you get into the detail.

What?

If you prefer to **get to grips with a theory** before you start implanting it in practical situations, do the opposite. **Read through the theory once or twice before reading any case examples or questions**. Maybe cover it once using a text, once using a computer-based learning package. When you feel that you have nailed the theory - then look to see how it applies in practice and in the exam.

Learning styles action points

Now that you have identified your intelligences and your preferences for receiving information, you should do several things:

- ▶ Note your preferences
- ▶ Read through the rest of this book to see how you can **apply** your preferences to your studies
- ▶ Note which of your intelligences you are not using
- ▶ Consider whether you should try and develop any of them (using the exercises given previously)

Learning
styles

Types of
subject

Study
environment

Study
skills

Revision

Types of
question

Exam
paper

An
assortment

Types of
subject

Introduction

Having looked at how you learn in the last chapter, in this chapter we're going to move onto what you will be learning.

Accountancy exams are designed to equip you with the **knowledge** and **skills** necessary to perform well at increasing levels of responsibility.

Framework of exams

Exams are organised within a framework that reflects different levels of responsibility. There are variations in the framework used by different accounting bodies; the example below is the most common and it illustrates the progression of skills that all bodies aim to achieve.

1 Foundation level papers examine the core skills (such as use of procedures, methods and communication) that everyone working as an accountant should have

2 Intermediate level papers test more advanced technical topics that someone in a senior role would have to know, and also involve more complicated situations

3 Final or strategic level papers are primarily concerned with managerial skills such as problem solving and developing strategy

The subjects you'll be studying

The second half of the chapter is devoted to the most important subject areas for exams. We won't be using a lot of jargon in these pages, but we shall show you the main things you have to do to pass.

This chapter will demonstrate what you need to achieve in your studies.

We shall look at each level in more detail over the next few pages.

What we'd like you to do when you read the remaining chapters of this book is remind yourself constantly what you need to demonstrate to the examiner. Ask yourself how different study skills and revision techniques can help you pass.

Are you worried about coping with subjects that involve lots of numbers?

or

Are you concerned about having to write lots of essays for certain subjects?

If you answered yes to either question, turn to page 31.

Foundation exams

The entries in the accounting records have to be organised and summarised if they are to be useful to the accountant.

The hows

The basic skill that you'll learn at Foundation level is how to make entries in accounting records. You will also learn how to use information contained in those records.

▶ Classifying information into different categories
▶ Aggregating and summarising information by preparing accounts

And the whys

Foundation exams will also give you an introduction into the theory of accountancy. This involves becoming familiar with accounting terminology. You will also need to have some knowledge of wider accounting concepts that influence how you treat and interpret information.

This will be a fundamental point throughout your studies; learning a technique means learning how to use it intelligently, not unthinkingly.

Similarly, learning techniques at this level is not just about learning a series of mechanical processes. Even at this stage, you need to develop a critical understanding of what you are doing.

▶ When you should use the techniques
▶ The limitations of the techniques

Examination methods

Most Foundation level exams these days will test you by means of multiple choice or short answer (objective test) questions. You may well sit computer-based exams; we shall cover these later in this book. Papers that require longer answers will examine your communication skills, presenting information logically and clearly in various formats.

You may be asked to
▶ State (express or detail clearly)
▶ Describe (communicate key features)

Exemptions

If you are taking certain qualifications, you may be exempt from some or all of the lowest level papers. However when you study higher level papers, you will be expected to know topics that were covered at Foundation level. You may therefore have to spend time studying these areas before moving onto more advanced topics, in particular in the core subjects of financial accounting and management accounting.

Intermediate exams

More ability

You will be expected to have more expertise than at Foundation level. Therefore you have to learn about more complex topics and more advanced techniques, applied to more complicated situations.

More analysis

You will also find out more about how data is used in the planning, control and decision-making processes. You will use a range of measures, financial and non-financial, to judge performance.

More authority

The papers will test how skilful you are in various aspects of a supervisory role.

- ▶ Exercising control
- ▶ Designing, managing and evaluating systems
- ▶ Interpreting results, identifying problems and deciding how they will be investigated

The way forward

You will also start to find out about the wider strategic decisions businesses make, which you will study further at final level, in particular certain critical choices.

- ▶ Sources of finance
- ▶ Investment decisions

At Foundation level the techniques you have to use will normally be clearly signposted. The situations you encounter at Intermediate level will not be so clear cut (more like real-life in fact).

Exams will test how good you are at supervising day-to-day operations, and how you can contribute effectively to project development.

Key techniques

Making a big effort to grasp techniques will not only secure you a pass at Intermediate level, but will also benefit you at Final level, where many techniques learned at Intermediate level will be needed again.

Final exams

Examples of key decisions

- ▶ *Merging/taking over other companies*
- ▶ *Managing business risks*

Key skills

- ▶ *Linking different techniques*
- ▶ *Bringing in material from other subjects*
- ▶ *Using knowledge of the local and international business environments*
- ▶ *Discussing developments and controversies*

The ultimate test

Most final level exams will test how you would cope in a senior management role, taking key business decisions. In some subjects you will not be an employee of the organisation described in the question; you will however be in a equivalent senior role, a business adviser or audit partner for example.

The wide strategic perspective

You will have to show that you can recommend and justify strategic decisions, concerned with the overall long-term direction of organisations. These decisions will demand awareness of the internal and external situation, also the implications of organisations' mission and goals. You will need to think widely about the problems organisations face and demonstrate commercial awareness.

How you're examined

Often in final level papers you will be given a business situation that reflects, or is drawn from, real-life examples. You will have to use selectively the knowledge, theory, calculations and techniques you have learned at lower levels to analyse the information you are given and make recommendations. This involves more than just describing what you know: it means gaining insight on the data in the question by using the knowledge and skills that you have.

You will be writing reports that will be read by recipients specified in the question; what you write must be tailored to your readership's needs and demands.

Remember

that you will primarily be tested on your ability to provide realistic business advice, with less emphasis on technical knowledge than at earlier stages.

Words and numbers

You may have one of two views on how your studies will go.

1 You feel that the written papers should not be too demanding, but you will struggle with papers involving lots of calculations, as you've never been very good at maths.

2 You don't think you'll have any problems with the numbers, but you've always found writing long essays more challenging. You're used to doing your written work on computer, and will find writing for three hours on paper challenging.

If you're unhappy with the calculations ...

Most of the techniques you will use in accountancy papers are not mathematically difficult; it's more a case of knowing the steps to follow. The final answer to long calculations needn't be correct for you to pass; what you must remember is that you can gain sufficient marks by getting certain stages right.

If you're unhappy with the essays ...

Examiners rarely complain that students cannot express themselves in words. More common sources of complaint are answers being untidy and lacking a clear layout, and answers containing irrelevant material.

The way to gain confidence in writing answers on paper is to practise. You should spend time not just answering individual questions against the clock, but also complete exams in three hours.

Key steps are:

▶ Do the easy calculations

▶ Set out your workings clearly

▶ Discuss the results of your calculations and their limitations

You needn't be a wordy (linguistic) person to set your work out well, write in clear and complete sentences and answer the question being asked.

Remember

that you will see **lots** of questions that require you to carry out calculations **and** provide commentary.

In final level papers the question may include numerical data which you are expected to use in calculations, even if the question requirements don't specifically require you to carry out calculations.

The subjects you'll study

Bear in mind that you'll study certain subjects at more than one level. You'll also need to think about why you encounter subjects at some levels but not others.

Active review

In chapter 4 we shall talk about how you should review the material you have learned so that you can recall it better. Review can just mean reading through your notes again. However answering a question or doing an exercise is normally a much better test of how well you have understood what you have studied.

That's an introduction to an exercise we'd like you to do. We've listed below eight main subject areas that are tested in the exams of most or all accountancy bodies.

- Financial accounts (for shareholders/external users)
- Auditing (checking the truth and fairness of accounts)
- Management accounts (for internal managers)
- Financial management
- Information technology
- Management
- Tax
- Law

For each subject area

- State the learning styles covered in chapter 1 that you think will be of greatest assistance when studying the subject

In the next part of this chapter, we shall give you some answers for this exercise, and also provide you with an indication of the main themes that run through each subject.

Top tips

We shall also include a tip that will help you study more effectively. Bear in mind that most of the tips apply to more than one subject. For example, finding out common mistakes students keep making (the tax tip) will benefit you in other subjects as well.

Financial accounting

Financial accounts are monetary statements summarising an organisation's performance during a period and its position at the period-end. You will have to prepare accounts in a variety of formats according to rules laid down in law and accounting standards.

Examples of typical financial accounting questions are 'Prepare a set of group accounts' or 'Prepare a cash flow statement in accordance with International Financial Reporting Standard 1.'

However you will also need to understand the logic behind the accounting rules so that you can explain the treatment of items within accounts. For higher level papers, you may have to criticise current or proposed regulations.

An example would be 'Discuss the current problems relating to the treatment of leases in financial statements.'

You will also have to examine accounts and interpret the messages they give, highlighting the aspects of most interest to readers.

You might be asked to prepare a report for the chairman of a group of companies, comparing the business and financial performance of two companies within the group.

This is likely to be good news for bodily-kinaesthetic people.

Intrapersonal people should find this aspect interesting.

People with musical abilities should enjoy trying to identify patterns within a set of data.

Balance Sheet

Top tip

Remember that financial accounting papers can be wide-ranging; even if you do find the preparation of certain types of accounts difficult, don't spend **all** your time practising them. You need to ensure that you can answer other questions that do not involve the preparation of accounts.

Auditing

Hence you need to be able to decide which audit tests are relevant for the client's circumstances, and if necessary, devise some of your own; this may appeal if you are a bodily kinaesthetic person.

Auditors look to gather evidence by reviewing a business's accounts and records so that they can give an opinion. External auditors, who are not employees of the company, give opinions on the reliability of accounts.

Often in questions your role will be the senior member of the external audit team on site, responsible for the detailed work being completed. You will therefore have to decide how best to gain evidence about the organisation's systems, transactions, assets and liabilities.

A typical question will give you details that relate to an audit area, and ask what you need to find out about that area and the audit procedures you will use.

Questions also reflect the need for you to follow up problems if you find them, and to act professionally and ethically in sensitive situations.

Dealing with clients effectively doesn't just mean quoting the auditing rulebook every time there's a problem; it also involves the use of interpersonal skills.

You might be asked what you need to investigate in a particular situation, or to describe what you should do when your firm is threatened with removal from office as an auditor.

For higher level papers, you will be asked about more complicated audits, also assignments other than audits. You will also have to show that you can take the kind of management decisions that audit partners (in overall charge of the external audit) would take.

These include decisions about whether to accept appointment as an auditor and on overall audit strategy for a particular client.

Top tip

Give sufficient detail of what is being audited, explain what is being audited and why. For example don't just say:

“ Check expenditure is correctly stated ”

SAY

“ **Check expenditure is correctly stated by comparing payments in the cash book with purchase invoices and other supporting documentation** ”

Management accounting

Understanding why different types of data (above all cost data) are important is fundamental in management accounting. You will learn about various ways of classifying, analysing and using data.

Although a lot of these techniques can be learned as a step approach, you will also need to understand why different methods are used, and in what circumstances; remember at higher levels you will have to select the best techniques yourself.

For intermediate level papers, you will study techniques that are used for the purpose of controlling the organisation. These include planning, resource allocation and investigation of variations from what was expected. As you are promoted, you will become accountable for how your department performs; you therefore need to understand the significance and limitations of various performance measures.

A lot of questions will involve setting budgets, or considering how actual performance differed from the standards that should have been achieved.

Your management accounting skills will ultimately be used to assess the effects of strategic decisions, including decisions about pricing, product ranges and marketing.

You may be asked to discuss the decisions and the methods that can be used to measure whether the goals set have been achieved.

We mentioned earlier that accountancy is like a language. Management accountants have to explain the meaning of the data they use to non-financial decision-makers. They may also have to make assumptions on the basis of imperfect information and be aware of the limitations of the data.

Bodily-kinaesthetic people might enjoy applying these techniques.

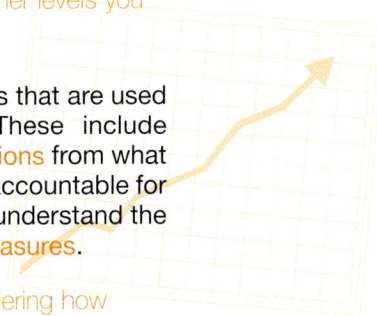

An important aspect of management accounting measures is how they affect people's behaviour, so interpersonal skills will be useful here.

Top tip

Remember always to do every part of each question! A common theme in examiners' reports in management accounting papers is candidates spending all their time on calculations, and not attempting question parts involving written discussion.

Financial management

Finance is a vital element in business planning and decision-making, and financial management therefore covers many of the key decisions businesses make. At the heart of this subject are the sources of finance businesses have available, the management of these sources and how the finance available affects business decisions.

> Questions range from considering the appropriateness of various finance sources to assessing the consequences of choosing different mixes of finance.

At intermediate level you will study day-to-day management of cash and other current assets and liabilities.

> The main current assets and liabilities are goods held in stock, balances owing from customers, and balances owed to suppliers.

You will also learn how to value companies and to appraise investments. These techniques are then used to support decision-making at higher levels, when you will examine the impact of major investment decisions upon business strategy.

> A very common subject of questions is whether one company should buy another company.

Another important topic is how businesses manage financial risks that could seriously threaten their existence. These include the risk of important sources of finance no longer being available, also the risks businesses face from adverse exchange or interest rate movements.

Thus financial management is not a mechanical subject, but involves the intrapersonal skill of thinking through the implications of major decisions.

Maths logical people may enjoy calculating the impact of different risk management policies.

Top tip

Financial management is not just a textbook subject; regular reading of the business pages of newspapers will provide real-life examples of the decisions and factors you will be discussing when considering financial strategy.

We'll look more at reading business pages in the Chapter on Study Skills.

Information systems

Information systems papers are not primarily about details of the latest technological developments.

Although you do need to know about commonly used hardware and software, you must also appreciate what qualities information needs to possess (this is also essential for the accounting papers).

Information systems are very important, reflecting the fact that you must be aware of the information you need to do your job. As well as the design and development of information systems, you will also be tested on their implementation, control and evaluation.

A typical question would cover the various stages of a systems project.

Exams for higher level papers focus on the part information systems play in the strategic management of the organisation. You will learn how information technology is changing the nature and structure of the working environment, and how use of information systems can give businesses competitive advantages.

You will often be given a business situation that has several aspects which you need to discuss. You would not only consider the links between information and business strategy, but wider managerial and environmental issues as well.

Spatial-visual people should cope well with questions that cover construction of systems, and what systems are needed for particular environments.

Mathematical-logical people may be able to spot system flaws!

Top tip

Do not spend too much time mastering the technical intricacies of computer systems, however interesting you find them. The exams are not designed to turn you into an information technology specialist. Examiners often complain that higher level answers contain too much technical detail, and not enough discussion on how information technology can be used to fulfil a business's objectives.

Management

Management papers test your ability to take decisions and solve problems. The management theory and the analysis methods that you study will help you develop solutions.

Ultimately you will be studying strategic management, the development, implementation and control of strategies.

Management papers at intermediate level tend to concentrate on matters affecting business operations. These include human resources, relationships within an organisation and management culture. Management of change is also very important.

Examples of problems that you might encounter include introducing effective recruitment policies, or taking steps to overcome resistance to change.

At the highest levels you will be required to evaluate strategic options, bearing in mind the consequences of, and constraints upon, the various options. You will have to apply relevant theory to the organisation described.

Most higher level papers include compulsory longer questions. You will be given a lot of detail about an organisation and have to provide recommendations for future strategy.

Management papers will also test skills and knowledge you have learned in other papers. These include use of financial information and performance measurement criteria to evaluate strategy, and the impact of technological developments.

Both intrapersonal (thinking a problem through to its solution) and interpersonal (where you appreciate the human dimension) skills are important here.

The spatial visual skill of being able to visualise the environments within which strategies will be developed will be useful.

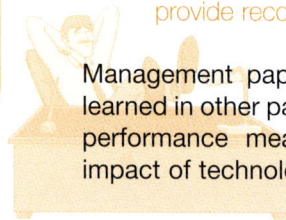

Top tip

Remember that no management model is applicable in all circumstances. You will have to select the most appropriate model and apply it to the question where relevant. A good way of developing your skill at doing this is whenever you've learnt a model or theory, think of three or four different kinds of organisation and consider the problems in applying the model or theory to those organisations.

There is rarely a right or wrong answer in management questions, especially at higher level.

Tax

Tax is an important topic in accountancy exams, as most people in general accounting roles will deal with some tax issues; tax is not always left to specialists. All managers need an appreciation of the tax impacts of decisions they are taking.

Most accountancy bodies first examine tax at intermediate level. You will need to know the detailed technical rules, and be able to apply them in calculating tax and possibly reporting your findings. The most important technique in tax papers is the tax computation.

> Calculating the tax individuals or companies owe on their income is at the heart of tax papers.

Higher level papers will require you to act as a tax adviser. This will involve understanding your clients' objectives at various stages of their lives, and recommending strategies that will result in tax charges being avoided or deferred. The onus will be on you to recognise which taxes are relevant.

> You may therefore be asked to assess the suitability of different courses of action, bearing in mind the tax consequences of each and the personal or business circumstances of your client.

Tax will often appeal to maths logical people who enjoy carrying out long calculations, following a set of prescribed rules.

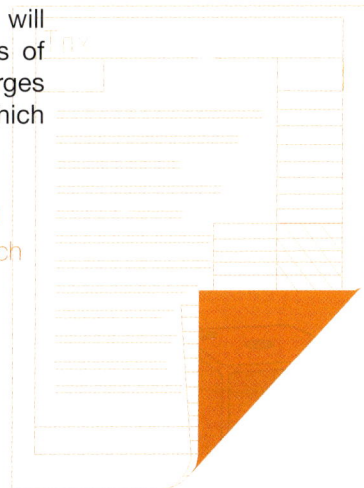

Top tip

Examiners' reports offer a good guide to aspects of tax that candidates get wrong sitting after sitting after sitting. Knowing what these are and making sure you get them right can **significantly** enhance your chances of passing.

Law

Accountants need to be able to recognise issues of legal significance when they encounter them in their day-to-day work, even though they are not being trained as lawyers. Hence law has always formed part of accountancy syllabuses.

Law is now often tested at Foundation level, the main aim being to test knowledge, in particular breadth of knowledge.

Hence law at this level is often tested by means of multiple-choice or other short answer questions. The more questions there are, the greater the number of areas of law that can be tested, and the greater the assurance gained that students who pass the exam have sufficiently wide-ranging knowledge.

Where law is examined at intermediate level, some questions will ask you to outline features of the legal system or state a body of law.

For example you may be asked to explain the importance of the courts in the legal system, or what details company documents should contain.

You may however be given questions which require the skills of being able to recognise legal problems, apply the law to the situation described and communicate your analysis to interested parties.

These will involve fictional scenarios with details that are similar to one or a number of decided cases, where a number of legal points arise.

> *Linguistic people may enjoy studying the detail that you need to know to do well in law.*

> *Scenario questions will call upon intrapersonal skills, the ability to think issues through to a conclusion.*

Top tip

For law papers where questions come in a variety of formats, you need to find out how different areas are most likely to be tested. Specific rules will often be tested by multiple-choice questions, areas where the main law is statute-based by 'state the law' type questions, and areas where there is a lot of case law by fictional scenarios. Law is not primarily about learning lists of case names and section numbers; you need to know that points of law arose in a decided case, and what the main legislation was called, but you don't need to know all the sub-paragraph numbers.

General papers

General papers are set by some examinining bodies as Foundation and Final level exams.

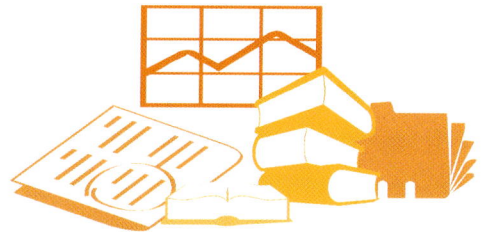

General papers may be underpinned by a particular theme. Questions may for example be based on a single subject, such as different events in a business's lifecycle. Alternatively the theme may impact upon your approach to answering questions. In a paper on business risks and controls, you will look out in question scenarios for the range of risks organisations face, and discuss how they can manage and control these risks.

Foundation papers are often broadly based round the business environment, designed to test that you have the breadth of general knowledge necessary to support analysis and discussion at higher level. As with law at Foundation level, the methods of testing used (generally short answer questions) are designed to cover as much of the syllabus as possible in every exam.

Final level general papers cover a variety of the subjects we have covered in this chapter. Breadth of knowledge is again important; many students struggle because they concentrate too much on certain knowledge areas. Examiners also wish to test how you react to unanticipated data and question requirements, so you must be prepared for surprises in the exam.

The ultimate general paper is the Case study. You will not have to learn anything new for this paper. Instead you will be faced with an unstructured business situation and collection of data; you will use the knowledge you already have only where you can add value. We shall look at Case study questions in detail in the chapter on types of question.

Top tip

Examiners of final level general papers will expect you to bring in relevant knowledge and skills from exams you have already sat at lower levels and other higher level exams. Be prepared to use what you know, but always in the context of the general paper. Using your knowledge from other papers to support your answer briefly should gain you marks; a long digression into detailed technical areas from other papers won't help you pass.

Learning
styles

Types of
subject

Study
environment

Study
skills

Revision

Types of
question

Exam
paper

An
assortment

Study
environment

Study environment

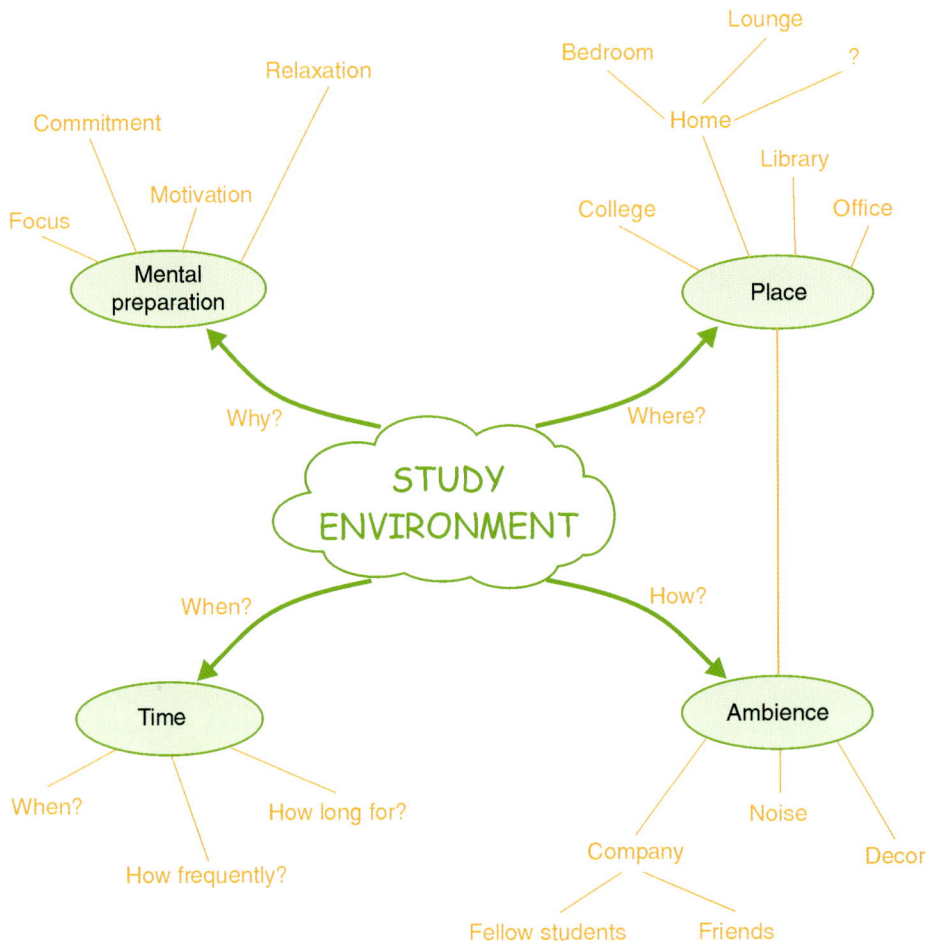

The mind map shows STUDY ENVIRONMENT in a central cloud with four branches:

Why? → Mental preparation: Focus, Commitment, Motivation, Relaxation

Where? → Place: College, Home (Bedroom, Lounge, ?), Library, Office

When? → Time: When?, How frequently?, How long for?

How? → Ambience: Company (Fellow students, Friends), Noise, Decor

Introduction

The mind map above outlines the factors that make up this Chapter. Having previously looked at how you prefer to receive and process information, and having taken a look at the nature of the subjects you are likely to have to study, we shall now explore the environment in which you study.

Mental preparation

In the next few pages we are going to address four aspects of being mentally prepared for your accountancy studies. Perhaps the most important is motivation. When setting yourself out to do something you are aware will be challenging, it is important to be clear in your own mind why you are doing it.

We will also touch on commitment. The nature and timetable of any accountancy exams mean that you have made a big commitment to your training. This is closely linked with motivation. You have made the commitment because you want to achieve the goal: qualification.

It is wrong to concentrate too much on the difficulties of training. We don't want to put you off! It is also important to relax into studying, as your brain works better when it is relaxed, so we will look a little at the question of relaxation.

Lastly, we shall look at focus, which is strongly linked with the other aspects of mental preparation discussed.

Motivation
Commitment
Relaxation
Focus

Why?

Training to be an accountant is a tough task - don't let anyone tell you differently.

Anyone who has trained as an accountant would tell you they had days when the WHY of training to be an accountant loomed large and they were not sure how to answer it.

If you have started out on this course then there is no doubt that you have made a substantial commitment to your career, and to a certain way of life for a period of time.

It is therefore very important that you prepare yourself mentally for the prospect of both training and studying to be an accountant.

This book deals in the main with the studying side, in practice you will find that the two overlap.

Were you ever a boy scout or girl guide? When facing training as an accountant, it is a good idea to borrow the scouts' motto:

Be prepared

Motivation

Take a moment to think, and then jot down the reason (s) why you are studying to be an accountant, in the space given below.

Was this a cinch for you? Do you have a clear idea of why you have got yourself into this, or was it quite hard for you to identify why you are doing it?

Whatever the reason you have written down in the box to the left is, it is unlikely that you have written nothing. Getting a place on a course to study accountancy, or a training contract with a firm of accountants is not an easy thing to do, so you must have put some effort into it. That type of effort rarely comes without a reason.

Sometimes people go into things because they couldn't think of anything better to do. That is **not a good reason**. That will **not motivate you** through at least three years of hard work in your (sometimes minimal) spare time and a string of challenging exams. You had better re-think your reason quickly.

Studying is easier if your brain wants to learn. It is very important to be motivated to learn. Motivation is a key learning tool. It will help to improve your concentration, and it will drive your commitment to your studies. A key part of preparing to learn is identifying your motivation. You have just done that in the box to the left.

Training to be an accountant takes a long time. It can be easy to forget this motivation. Your motivation may change or waver over the coming months and years. You may think our next suggestion is the most stupid thing that you have ever heard, or you may think that it will be helpful. It's up to you:

Write out your motivation on a sheet of paper and tack it above your desk, carve it into your pencil case and put it in your diary.

KEEP IT with you.
You will **NEED IT.**

Motivation

"I want to qualify and have my own independent practice."

"I want to command a good salary with great prospects"

"I've always wanted to be an accountant - now I've got all the right grades so far and a place with a training firm, so I'm really going to go for it!"

Commitment

Commitment

Commitment **stems from motivation** and has a strong link with **time management,** which we will look at later in this Chapter.

MOTIVATION
I want this

COMMITMENT
Therefore I will put time into it ...

Relaxation

TENSE BRAIN = NOT COOPERATIVE

Scientists have proved that a relaxed brain is more receptive to learning than a tense one. Trust me, it is something to do with neurones, electricity, brain waves, synapses or something ... Let's leave the science to the scientists and just enjoy the fact that from now on, despite the fact that we are studying, we have to make sure that we are relaxed.

Several things have an impact on relaxation:

1 Time (see page 57)   Schedule **time off.**
Schedule study time **sensibly.**

2 Ambience (see page 54)   **Know** what helps you to relax **before** you sit down to study.

3 Support   The support **BPP** offers is discussed below.

You will also require the support of your friends and family. You may have to ask them to help out with things such as creating a good study atmosphere, giving you time to study and so on…

Support from BPP

If you are booked on a BPP Home Study or Classroom course and you are tense about your study, do not suffer in silence. BPP offers on-line and telephone support for when you do not understand an element of your studies. **Call, discuss, relax...**

Focus

Concentration checklist

Movement

When you sit down to study are you in a place that you can work peacefully in? Or are you going to be disturbed (for example, if you work on the kitchen table, or the bus…)? Movement is likely to break up your concentration.

Vision

When you sit down to study are you in a place with nothing very interesting to look at? Or are things going to catch your attention (for example if you sit by a window, or opposite the front door)? Your eyes will be drawn - end of concentration. See page 55

Temperature

When you sit down to study are you in a place that is unusually hot or cold, or where the temperature will fluctuate? You will have personal preferences about temperature, but changes in it may adversely affect your concentration. See page 55

Noise

When you sit down to study, do you have control over the noises you hear, or is the place noisy? (For example, you control the music in your own room, but not the traffic on the street.) Uninvited noise may affect your concentration. See page 55

Intentions

When you sit down to study do you have a clear work plan in your head, or are you just sitting at your desk so you don't feel guilty? It is much easier to concentrate if you have planned a task to carry out. See page 54

Focus is strongly connected to all the things we have considered so far in this Chapter.

- ▶ *Motivation*
- ▶ *Commitment*
- ▶ *Relaxation*

All help you focus.

Concentration is an important aspect of focus. Concentration is affected by:

- ▶ *Where you study*
- ▶ *When you study*
- ▶ *How you study*

We will be going on to consider all these things now.

You need to know what helps you concentrate and what disturbs your concentration.

You may find it helpful to work through the concentration checklist on the left.

Your concentration

List five things that ...

Stop you concentrating

Help you to concentrate

Place

Where?

As we touched on in the first Chapter, if you are training to be an accountant, then it is probable that you are learning in more than one location.

*You are undertaking **practical training** at your office. You are probably being given **teaching** at a college or training company.*

*Lastly, and importantly in this book, you will be **studying privately** and trying to learn the mechanics of what you have been taught and have experienced.*

The 'Where?' in this book is going to concentrate largely on where you would best study privately, as the questions of where you are taught, and where you receive practical training will largely be decided for you.

'Where?' is a difficult question to address in a book for the following reasons:

▶ Everyone's circumstances are different
▶ Generalisations can be unhelpful
▶ It is a matter of personal preference
▶ It may be a matter you feel you have little control over

However, think through the following issues:

1 Honesty. Own up if you know you study in a place which is not conducive to study for any reason (you don't really want to study/you get lonely studying when everyone else is having fun/it is more comfortable on the bed…)

2 Choice. You may not think that you have many choices about where you can study, but look at the list of options you could consider (given below).

3 Relaxation and balance. Remember that the tense brain is uncooperative, so study in a place where you can relax (just remember to be honest about the balance between relaxation and concentration.) For example, if you hate libraries, don't make yourself go to one…

Study options

Some of these may be silly, but what about:

Public library, local café in its quiet period, local cricket match, the attic, granny's front room, a spare room at your college, the park, your office after everyone's gone home/got in, local church, late night trains, local curry house before 11.30 pm

It depends what you are trying to get away from…

I find

I used to work in front of the television when I really didn't want to be working. This was a lose-lose situation, because I neither watched the television properly, nor got any work done. If you recognise yourself doing this, compromise. Do an hour's work in quiet instead of two in front of the television. Then watch the programme.

College

If you want to find a quiet place to study, your office has a 24 hour culture and it's not easy to find a quiet corner at home, have you considered whether it would be possible for you to study before or after hours at your college?

Ask the following questions:

1 Is it possible that I could stay after class and make use of the room?

2 What hours is the college open?

3 If not, is there another room or a library I could use?

4 Does anyone mind if I do that, and should I let anyone know I am here?

Library

Unless where you live is very remote, you probably have access to a public library. This is another place that you can consider taking your study too.

However, public libraries aren't always everyone's cup of tea. They can be noisy, and they do not always come fitted with desks and places to study unless they are in big cities.

There may be other options.

The association you are training to be a member of may have a library.

Alternatively . . .

Is there a library at your office?

This probably only applies to larger firms, but if there is one, make sure you make full use of it, if you want to vary the place where you study.

Your office

Your office is probably plentifully supplied with large desks. What a shame that they go to waste for certain hours in every 24. **Study the culture of your office or department and consider whether you could make use of your office as a place of study**. Everyone may work late, but no one normally comes in before 9am. Could you bear to get up an hour earlier to come in and get some study done before anyone else is there? (Check what time the building opens first!) Alternatively, it may have an early culture, but there are always some desks free in a quiet area by 5.30pm. Could you bear to stay for an hour or so and take advantage of this solitude?

An advantage of studying at work if you can is that there is a clear distinction between where you work (work) and where you relax (home).

Home

Everyone's home is different and will have different features and spaces for you to put yourself in. But here are some ideas:

Attic

Having a loft conversion is probably beyond your pocket, but if you are desperate for peace and quiet, give your

Study

This is a fantastic number one place to study, if you can use it whenever you like and it's not filled with someone else's work. It is probably also the room most unlikely to exist in most people's houses.

If you do have a study, set yourself up a desk, computer and shelving, create an atmosphere which relaxes you and go for it!

Kitchen

It is probably less than ideal to work in a kitchen. The table might be nice and big, but there are too many potential distractions. You may feel tempted to stop working and start eating or drinking, and food and drink are easily accessible in the kitchen.

It is also a place where other people are likely to go if you don't live alone. Someone will need to cook the dinner, or your flatmates will want to get beer out of the fridge...

Which room?

Think through the key factors:

Are you alone?

(cont)

roof some consideration. Is there unused space up there you could board up and fill with a desk?

Bedroom

If you are living at your parents' home, or lodging with someone, this may be your best option. Is there room for a desk in your room? If not, you may find that, although pricey, an investment in some space saving furniture may pay dividends. For example, the IKEA* catalogue contains some ideas such as 'loft beds'. You may like to work in bed, and while previously we have advised you to work where you are relaxed and comfortable, it may not be advisable to work in bed. If trying to write (and, as we shall discuss in Chapter 4, this will be necessary) you are likely to get uncomfortable. This will break your concentration and encourage you to stop.

Living room

The living room may be a good place to work if there is room for a table. However, it is also a room in which people socialise, and this may not be at one with your need to concentrate and study. Be honest with yourself. Are you really going to concentrate on economics or financial decisions while your friends/family/flatmates are watching Eastenders? Are they going to appreciate you trying to?

If you do try and work in a living room, you are going to have to be very disciplined in your approach to your work, and also considerate to anyone who is trying to use the room for its proper purpose.

Have you got enough space?

Do you have a desk?

* BPP should point out, of course, that they don't hold shares in IKEA. The authors just shop there sometimes . . .

Ambience

The question of 'how' to approach your studies, that is, the type of study skills you will require, is looked at in Chapter 4, Study Skills.

The question 'how?' in this Chapter is really **an extension of the question 'where?'.** It is still looking at the environment in which you are going to study, but looks at peripheral things, such as the walls you are looking at, your movement during study, the temperature in your room, the things you can hear.

These may not seem as important as the question of where you study, but they are. And in actual fact, **they will probably impact significantly on how you choose the place you study** - remember how we said you might not want to work in the kitchen, because of various peripheral things, such as movement, people and heat?

How?

Scholars and educators will debate the relevance and importance of things that we are going to look at in the next few pages.

In our opinion, these things are only as important as they seem to be to you. If they matter to you, get them right!

Over the next few pages we are going to make a few comments on how seemingly peripheral things may impact on your studies, in a good or bad way. We have already noted a few of them in our observations about concentration, and it is in that context that we revisit them here. The golden question is always: 'Does it adversely affect your concentration?' If the answer is yes, get rid of it!

In the past, there have been some rules about study, such as, 'you must study in silence'. We may invite you to break the rules, if you can honestly say that you are creating a study system for you that works.

What are we going to look at?

Temperature
Company
Vision
Noise

Intention

We have mentioned intention before. Do not cheat yourself. To study effectively (and probably more efficiently) you have to approach your study sessions honestly, with an intention of trying to learn.

Sound

People are usually divided on the question of whether silence when you study is a good idea. As ever, we think whatever honestly works for you is the best policy.

It is a good idea to distinguish between planned and unplanned noise, however. Unplanned noise, such as drills in the street, a car alarm, a clock ticking, can be very irritating, and will affect your concentration.

We advise: Take a quick look around your room before you start work and eliminate any potential sources of irritating noise before you start. You should also take a quick look out of the window. If workmen are massing, can you go and work at the back of the house?

However, planned noise, particularly music, may have a beneficial effect on your study. Experts have shown that a quality in Baroque music has a particularly beneficial effect on the brain, relaxing the brain to an optimum level. You obviously have to work within your own taste, though.

I find

Music helps me to relax into my study. However, I always know when it is not working, because I find that once I am concentrating, I can no longer hear the music - so if I can hear it, I'm not!.

Once I hear the music, I need to take a break.

Some people who are musical may find that playing music helps them to remember facts, because they associate the facts with the music in their head.

Vision

Your **sense of sight** is one of your more commonly used senses.

If your **eyes** are tired from reading, or from looking at your own handwriting, they will be **prone to distraction** by things around them.

You need to **consider what you can see** from your place of study, and to further consider whether it will distract you.

Some people advise you to sit in front of a **blank wall** in a **relaxing colour** (ie not fiery red), or a **beautiful scene**. Some keep the **motivation statement** we suggested on page 46 in front of them to look at if their attention wandered.

You know what distracts you. If it is a window, don't study next to one, etc ...

Temperature

People can generally tell you whether they like working in hot or cold temperatures. I prefer cold, **what do you prefer?** Then when you sit down to study, make sure the temperature is right.

Another important factor is **changes in temperature**. This is likely to be distracting. **If you can control the temperature, do**. Make sure the window is open/closed before you start, turn the radiator up or down. If you leave it, you may use it as an excuse to wander away from your study ...

Company

If you live alone, this may not be an issue which affects you unduly. For those who live with friends or family, company when studying can be a significant problem.

On the flip side of the coin, the company of people undertaking the same process as you can be very useful. Later we shall review the helpfulness of teaching in order to learn. As part of that, discussing issues arising from your study with a person who is also learning can be a helpful review, and an indicator of any problems that might have arisen.

Friends and family

Friends and family can be **extremely helpful** when you are studying accountancy (for example on those nights when you have three hours worth of study to do in one and a half hours and you haven't eaten all day, and someone has put the dinner on the table so you don't have to cook it yourself ...).

They can also be **extremely unhelpful**.

When you study, you will be seeking to **concentrate** on your work, and **avoiding distractions** which may take away from that concentration.

Friends can be extremely distracting. Unless you have very considerate friends, or friends who are in the same boat as you, friends may not understand why that person who used to be the life and soul of the party is now always found with their head in a book.

If you live with your friends, you might also find that they are very **noisy**. They might not mind being evicted sometimes, but will not be too keen on you asking them to keep it down all the time in their own home.

You need to strike a balance. You need to **explain** your position to people from the outset. You need to consider options such as **studying away from home on occasion** (at work, or in a library), investing in some **ear plugs**, and scheduling **guilt-free nights** out with your friends so that you don't turn into a complete hermit!

Study partners

The phrase **'study buddy'** may throw you into a tremendous squirm. However, you may find that discussing your study with someone else who is studying is a **very useful tool.** Alternatively you can make use of the virtual student discussion forums that many training providers now run.

Time

When?

In the next few pages we are going to address the question of When? We shall look at time. For the next three or four years, you may make some of the following observations:

> **There aren't enough hours in the day.**
>
> **Where has the last year gone?**
>
> **I have plenty of time until my exams ... whoops, where did it all go?**
>
> **I don't have time to do all the study I have to do this week.**
>
> **My manager doesn't understand. I've got a course exam next week, I can't possibly work overtime.**

You are going to have to learn to be **creative with time**.

Whatever your normal preference with regard to organising yourself is, to succeed in studying accountancy, you should learn how to timetable and plan your time. This does not have to be a formal process, but it can be if it helps.

Fleeting time ● ● ●

Think about how you have studied in the past and in particular, to what time frame you have studied. Would you sum yourself up as 'Last minute wonder' or 'Slow and steady wins racer'?

Please assess whether the following statements reflect your approach, using (1) as 'strongly reflects my approach' and (5) as 'does not reflect my approach' and (2) to (4) as degrees between these two positions.

Statement	(1)	(2)	(3)	(4)	(5)
1 I plan my work.	☐	☐	☐	☐	☐
2 My plans contain specific time deadlines.	☐	☐	☐	☐	☐
3 My plans incorporate time off from study.	☐	☐	☐	☐	☐
4 I never plan.	☐	☐	☐	☐	☐
5 I get to the week before exams and then spend a lot of time planning.	☐	☐	☐	☐	☐
6 I plan as a device to stop me starting working.	☐	☐	☐	☐	☐
7 I always plan 'lack of understanding gaps'.	☐	☐	☐	☐	☐
8 I don't plan initial work but always plan revision.	☐	☐	☐	☐	☐
9 I find plans constrictive because I don't know how I will respond to different topics.	☐	☐	☐	☐	☐
10 I think planning is a waste of time.	☐	☐	☐	☐	☐
11 I like to study for short periods, regularly.	☐	☐	☐	☐	☐
12 I like to save my effort for one big session.	☐	☐	☐	☐	☐
13 I prefer to work in the morning.	☐	☐	☐	☐	☐
14 I prefer to work in the evening.	☐	☐	☐	☐	☐
15 I can only work after midnight.	☐	☐	☐	☐	☐
16 I take lots of breaks.	☐	☐	☐	☐	☐
17 I can't study for two days in a row.	☐	☐	☐	☐	☐
18 I like to have a good run at work - do it for a week solid and then ignore it.	☐	☐	☐	☐	☐
19 I find it impossible to sit down and work unless the exams are looming.	☐	☐	☐	☐	☐
20 I find I go off like a train, but by the time the exams come round, I've forgotten it all.	☐	☐	☐	☐	☐

Analysis

You may not have needed the questionnaire to analyse your study style, but if it is a while since you last studied, a little prompting won't have hurt. Use the matrix below to analyse how you study.

What is your attitude to planning and timetabling your work?

When do you like to work?

... In a day?   **... In a course?**

Be prepared to change ● ● ●

One thing that this book is trying to do is get you to approach your studies in a way that it **tailor made** both **to you** and to **accountancy training**.

The best way to approach these exams may not be the same as the approach you took to other exams in the past, even if (a) that approach worked well in those circumstances, and (b) you have previously studied accountancy in some form, eg at university. You **may have to be prepared to change**, or **to adapt your style** to meet the challenges that this training has in store.

When?

The question of 'when?' will be strongly influenced by the method of teaching you choose or your firm buys for you. This may be a classroom course, or a course of Home Study.

BPP offers various types of courses for the differing professional qualifications (not all courses will be available for each qualification, if you are interested in attending a BPP course, please visit the BPP website at www.bpp.com). The key types of course are outlined here.

Full time The course lasts approximately 12 to 14 weeks with an average of 2-3 teaching days a week during the initial learning phase and an average of 4-5 teaching days during the revision phase.

Intensive courses All course material is taught in one or two intensive phases.

Link courses Courses are broken down into a number of discrete blocks with gaps away from BPP after each block.

Block release Classes are held over a number of days in a week. You will then have a break and then return for a second block of days. These courses are ideal if you have sufficient study leave.

Day release Classes are held on weekdays. You will only require one day per subject in any given week.

Evening courses Where students receive teaching for two nights a week over a certain period.

Weekend/Friday-Saturday courses Where students receive teaching for one/two days/weekend over a period.

Question 1

On this page and the next two, we are seeking to answer the first time question:

'WHEN?'

Even if you are attending classroom courses, it will always be necessary for you to undertake some work of your own - see our following up suggestions on the next page.

If you are using a BPP Home Study (distance learning) package or a Home Study PLUS package, you will receive a detailed study guide. You will also be given a timetable advising you when to undertake the various elements of the course. So BPP answer lots of the questions for you. You still need to consider when is best for you in terms of your daily schedule (am/pm?), your commitments to work or family and things like your holidays.

If you are going on a period of full-time or intensive tuition, then you are likely to have a period of months directed at study. While you are attending the classroom course part of the time, the tutors will direct you towards question practice. They will also provide suggestions about how to use the time if you have a 'break' period between the two blocks. You should plan how you use this time, and ask the relevant /when/ questions: am/pm?, commitments to work and family, holidays.

Under block release, day release, link tuition, evening or weekend courses, you will receive blocks of teaching over a period of time, separated by weeks in which you are expected to carry out some home study. Your tutors will give you some guidance over how to best use the times away from college. You should also plan yourself how to use them to your best advantage. These can be the times where you ensure that your understanding of what you have been taught is sound and you can go over areas which you find difficult until you have mastered them. We shall discuss study methods in Chapter 4. Here, remember that down periods between courses are opportunities, and apply the 'When?' checklist below.

Home study package

Intensive tuition

Split tuition

The 'When?' checklist

Constrained periods, remember ...

Do I study better in   the morning / early evening / late evening   my lunch hour?

When am I planning to go on holiday?   Not just before exams, preferably!

What family commitments do I have which will affect my study?   Putting the kids to bed, granny's 90th birthday weekend, weddings ...

Can I take unpaid study leave?

The teaching programmes outlined on this page are similar to the Link method in that you will receive a short burst of teaching and then have a period where you do not have any teaching. Your tutors will direct you about how best to use your time, but remember to use the time wisely to progress your understanding.

You need to consider the when checklist to decide how to link your periods of tuition with your private study, to maximise the potential of the periods when you are not at college.

Full-time or intensive

Block or day release or link

Block or day release or link courses give you one or more days' teaching a week over a period of several weeks. Your tutors will guide you, but ensure that you use the time between courses to clarify your understanding and undertake any work on the days when you are not at college. We advise you to consider sectioning a bit of your weekend to devote to study. You might also want to consider allocating it a weeknight. You may find that it is not productive to study on the nights of the days you have attended college.

Evening

If you are attending evening courses, then it is likely that you are working in the day time, so will have to keep your private study to other evenings and the weekends. If you are already at college two evenings a week, you might find using other evenings a strain. Perhaps allocating a portion of your weekend to study might be your best option.

Weekend

If you attend courses at weekends, the converse is true. You may have to allocate weeknights to following up your study and doing any work which your tutors have suggested.

Following up classroom teaching

We would add this general advice ...

Your tutors will advise you what work would be advisable between your attendance at BPP courses

In the 24 hours following a class, ensure that you just run through the things you were taught and check that nothing came up that you really didn't understand. If such things did arise, make a note of them. You can then take one of the following actions: **(1) Ask, (2) Review in detail in your own study programme, (3) Mixture of both**. If you leave this process too long, you may find that you forget what you didn't understand until much nearer the exams, when you may not have the time to improve your understanding.

How frequently?

Scientists have discovered that the brain is more likely to remember something if it is exposed to that thing frequently over a time period.

Your brain is more likely to recall the things you have been taught and have learned for your exam, if you expose your brain to it more than once. You are likely to have a study technique that exposes your brain to things at least twice: the first time when you gain or receive the information, and your revision time.

Experts on the brain would suggest that you should expose your brain to information at least six times. You could use the classroom follow up as another exposure, but might want to build more such recall exposures in to your week. That may mean if you are attending a weekly course that you look over the things you learned on a course three or four times between classes. If there is a long time between your first class and the exam, you might want to spread your recall exposures over that time period. However, the first few reviews should be close together. Reviewing the material in a different medium – listening to a CD or using a computer-based learning package – may help recall.

Building blocks

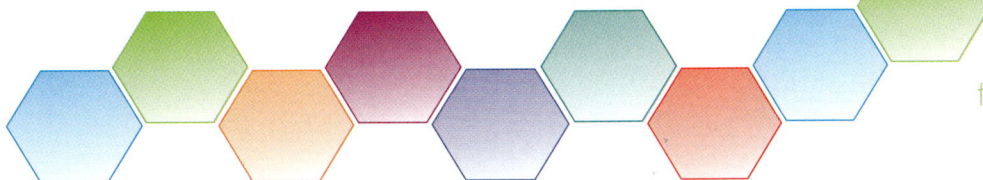

The other important consideration is that your study is set up like a set of building blocks. Something you are taught on one course, or you read in one study session is likely to underpin something you will meet in a future session.

Therefore, if your understanding of the foundations is limited, you will not be able to place the later blocks on your pile of learning. This may adversely affect your later performance.

Two things impact upon the question of how frequently, in addition to all the practical issues which we have raised when considering 'When?'.

The first is the review theory, which considers your brain recalls material. This will be important to you as you sit the exam hall, you can be sure of that!

The second is the way that your teaching is set up, both teaching you receive on classroom courses and the teaching you receive from BPP Study Texts or i-Learn CD-ROMs. We shall call this the building blocks theory.

Building blocks ● ● ●

Review things frequently to ensure that gaps are filled

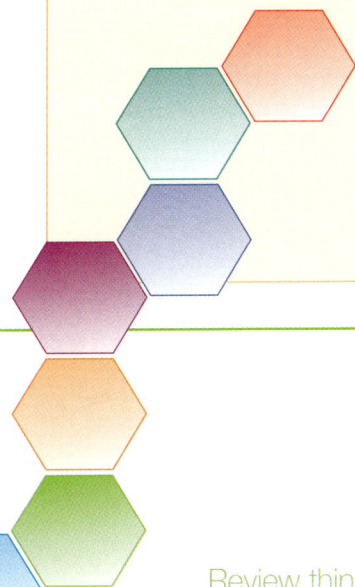

How long?

The question of how long will also be answered in part by the *practical restraints* on your time. You may have brief *'windows of opportunity'*, for example, your lunch hour or at 6 o'clock on Wednesday before swimming. In these instances, 'how long?' is answered for you - as long as you've got.

When choosing, consider the following issues:

▶ *That a series of shorter periods may prove more effective than one long study period*

▶ *The times of the day when you tend to be most alert; some people are morning people, some concentrate better in the evenings*

Whenever your best time is, it's important to plan when you're studying; it will help you commit to it.

Recall: primacy and recency

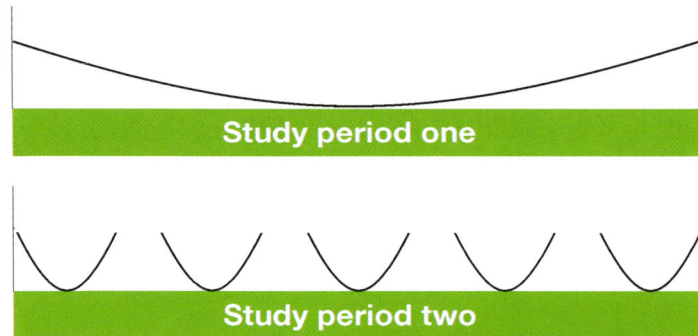

Study period one

Study period two

The diagram above shows two study sessions of the same length of time. The study period is illustrated in each case by the green block.

In the first study period, the student took no breaks. In the second, the student took four. Breaks are shown by the curved line being broken.

The diagram illustrates the concepts of primacy (you recall what happened first) and recency (you recall what happened most recently) - when the brain remembers best...

The brain recalls more easily things that you learn at a beginning or end of a session

To prove this, try and memorise a list of items, and analyse the result. You will recall a higher number of items at the beginning and end of each list.

Recall is shown in the diagram by the curved line. In study period one, the student recalls things more strongly from the start and end of the session (shown by the arrows). This is also true in study period, but they also recall things better from before and after each break which they took.

The outlook is good

Breaks are our friends, and we are positively encouraged to indulge.

But always remember:

> You must approach your study honestly. Taking breaks every five minutes because you don't really want to be studying at all will adversely affect your concentration. In other words, there won't be anything to recall! Take breaks sensibly and honestly

Also remember the important of **reviewing** the material, particularly that which is in the **recall dips**.

Learning
styles

Types of
subject

Study
environment

Study
skills

Revision

Types of
question

Exam
paper

An
assortment

Study
skills

Study skills

Points made so far ...

Teaching and learning are not the same thing.

A variety of skills are required to pass accountancy exams.

BUT ...

Don't let studying drive you mad!

This Chapter should help you create an effective approach.

The question of how to go about it may seem unanswerable! Be reassured; that is why this Chapter is here.

This Chapter looks at a variety of study skills and invites you to consider what methods suit you best. It will consider both types of information provision that are common in accountancy studies, lectures and home study. It is important for you to convert teaching into learning.

Another important piece of advice that this Chapter will give you is to think about the subject you are looking at before you dive in. In Chapter 2, the types of subject you will be studying were discussed. It is unlikely that you should approach them all in the same way. Tailor your approach…

Link

Remember back in Chapter 1, we discussed *learning styles*. Hopefully you worked through the illustrations that you were given there, and learnt a little about *how you prefer to study*.

This is the Chapter where that *self-awareness* will be the most useful, so you might want to *flick back* and *remind yourself* what you learnt.

Remember as you work through this Chapter, that knowing you *have two objectives to*:

1. *Discover* learning methods that suit you best and will facilitate your accountancy studies.

2. *Identify* study skills you do not like or find easy and try to *develop* them if necessary.

Chapter key

As this Chapter is closely linked with the learning styles Chapter, the following references are given when a skill is especially suited to a particular style.

Linguistic		Maths/logic	
Spatial/visual		Musical	
Interpersonal		Intrapersonal	
Bodily kinaesthetic			

Two stages of skills

The diagram shows a *brief outline* of the skills that we will be looking at in a great deal more detail in the rest of this Chapter.

The skills which are included in the *circle* are the same whichever course method you have taken, as they relate to work done after the course. Therefore, we shall deal with the skills relating to attending courses, and then move on to study skills used at home.

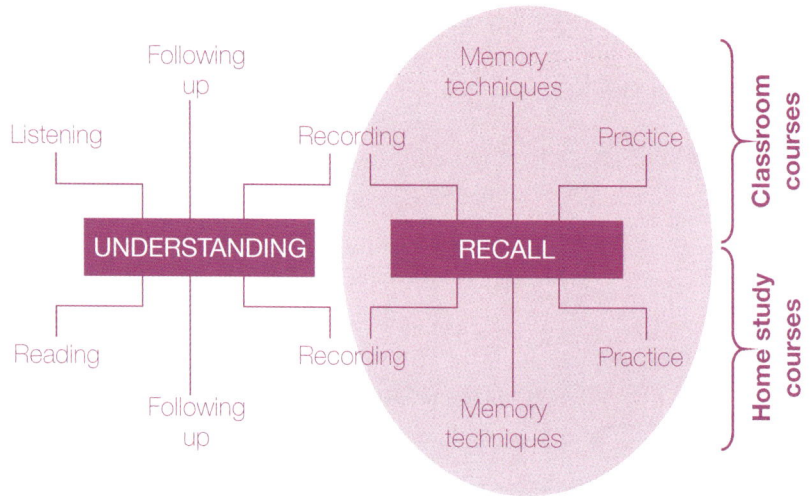

Following up

Listening   Recording   Practice

Memory techniques

UNDERSTANDING   **RECALL**

Classroom courses

Reading   Recording   Practice

Following up

Memory techniques

Home study courses

(a)	Listening		
(b)	Recording (1)		
(c)	Follow up (1)	STAGE 1 Classroom	
(d)	Reading		
(e)	Recording		STAGE 2 Home Study
(f)	Follow up (2)		
(g)	Recall		
(h)	Use		

Learning styles

Incidentally, just to ram home our point about learning styles, the diagram above has been produced in two styles. We think that the one on the top will appeal to spatial visual people and the one on the bottom will appeal to maths-logical people.

▶ Do you agree?
▶ Which one do you prefer?

Listening

Listening is an art of concentration. The ear is capable of hearing the noise being made by the tutor, even if there are other noises around. However to actually register what is being said, you have to concentrate.

Test it!

Go to a loud place, like an airport or a football match and try to have a conversation with someone. You will find that you can hear more than you think and that hearing increases as you concentrate.

If you find listening difficult, you might want to try out one or more of the following ideas:

1 **... Take notes** of what the lecturer is saying. Note taking is discussed on the next page in more detail. You will have to listen in order to write down what is being said.

I find ...
That I cannot concentrate on lectures at all unless I discipline myself to take notes on what is being said.

2 **... Tape the lecture** (with permission). Then you can listen to it again or even at your leisure.

3 **... Practise listening** Borrow some talking books from the library, follow a Parliamentary debate on television, use a BPP Success CD…

4 **... Know what distracts you and avoid it** at lectures (windows, the door, friends, noisy air conditioning units…)

A human person's healthy ear is amazing. We have an incredible capacity to *hear*.

However, as many parents or spouses observe, the capacity to *hear* and the capacity to *listen* are *not the same thing*.

People who noted in Chapter 1 that they were *aural people* will probably not find the skill of listening hard. Others may find that listening for extended periods of time is a chore.

If you are going to be given a lot of information aurally, then it is *important to learn how to listen*, or you may have to do a lot of work twice.

The wonder of hearing

" **I can always hear if my baby is crying,** it doesn't matter what else is going on ... "

" I always prick my ears up when people are talking about football. It's like I have radar or something ... "

Notetaking

The beauty of the second icon is that when you re-read the notes that you have made from the lecture and they don't make sense,

(a) YOU WON'T PANIC - they never made sense

(b) YOU KNOW TO ASK SOMEONE - follow up, (see the next page)

What to note down

Unless you know shorthand, you are going to be unable to write down everything that the lecturer says. In any case, to do so would be ineffective and wasteful.

A lecturer will repeat points to reinforce them, will give examples and further examples, will outline the background to topics which you have already covered and will teach you the essential things you need to know on a topic.

When making notes on a lecture, you need to note down the key points which the lecturer makes explaining the topic, and any examples that you find helpful.

Your own shorthand

In advance of a lecture, you should decide upon some simple shorthand of your own to save time. Here are two ideas to get you started:

▶ Abbreviate **key words**

This will save you time and make note taking easier.

> ### Example
> Management = mgmt or ☝

▶ Use **icons**

To highlight in the margin key points which the lecturer has made. You can use multiples of these to distinguish between important and absolutely vital…

To remind yourself of areas which confused you or you found difficult, or you were aware that you didn't understand as you were making the notes.

> ### Examples
>
> *
>
> !

Design your notes

You should also think carefully about what your notes look like, because that will affect how you review them and whether you use them properly in future.

Don't try and save paper - space out your notes to make them easier to read. This may involve:

▶   Double spacing your lines
▶   Not writing across the full page
▶   Frequent paragraphing

Use headers and boxes and circles and icons and pictures to identify key points.

Follow up

As we have noted above, handwritten notes are ad hoc notes, written at speed when listening to someone speaking.

You can convert these notes into useful revision material by typing them up on computer.

Another great beauty of the system is that the conversion process is itself a review, which is part of the learning process.

(a)   **Rewrite the notes** into notes that are coherent and flow properly, concentrating on the key points.

(b)   If you have a few !'s, think them through, or read around the subject to see if you can make sense of them. You may need to make a note to ask your lecturer about them when you next see him/her.

(c)   If you get to the end of a single lecture and you have lots of exclamation marks in your margin, check immediately what the problem is. There may be several issues, as highlighted here.

"Doesn't this all take too much time - why can't I just listen to the lecture?"

The question above is valid, because as we noted above, it is important not to be so devoted to your notes that you forget to listen to the lecture.

However, deciding in advance to double space your lines will not take time during the lecture and an asterisk only takes a second to scribble.

Try these note taking techniques and you might find that they become a vital part of an effective study system.

Potential causes of lots of !'s

1 You may need some 1 to 1 help on this topic.

2 You may have misunderstood something early which will make everything else make sense.

3 There may have been a problem with the lecture.

Reading

We are going to look at two things:

▶ **The skill of reading**
▶ **Approaching study materials**

The skill of reading

Reading is like many other skills, it improves with practice. If you hated reading when you were at school, then you probably gave it up to all intents and purposes when you left. Suddenly expecting yourself to be a genius at it again is asking a lot.

Of course, if you have always been a bookworm, you do practise regularly, and you probably could analyse an improvement over time.

Skill in reading is often measured in terms of time. People who think they are bad at reading moan 'I'm really slow.' In terms of reading, this is not necessarily a bad thing, although if you are studying, time is likely to be of the essence. However, the key skill in reading is comprehension. There is not much point reading, if you are not taking the information in…

1 Practise reading (things that interest you …)

Try the following:

▶ Keep a book or magazine (one with words, not pictures!) next to the toilet to peruse in a spare moment.

▶ Read all the adverts on the bus, train, tube or billboards on the way to work.

▶ Read the newspaper as you eat your breakfast.

Even if you think it's easy ● ● ●

Some people find reading very difficult and this fact can put them off their study even if they have fabulous memories or are otherwise well equipped. Others don't.

Even if you wonder what all the fuss is about, some of the suggestions made here about **how to approach study materials may be useful**.

2 Read out loud

If you find that you struggle to understand what you are reading, and you read things over several times to make sure that you have got them straight, try reading out loud for a little while. You might find that you respond better to hearing the words instead of seeing them.

Of course, reading things out loud often takes longer than reading them in your head, so this won't necessarily help your time management. So it might be best to save this technique for the most complex areas…

3 Read key words

BPP Study Texts are written to be concise, but to be in English, they have to include certain words that aren't necessarily vital.

Test it!

The cat sat on the mat.

If you read the above sentence, you know what the author is getting at. However, you would probably also get the idea if you read the following:

Cat sat mat.   Half of the sentence wasn't vital to your understanding!

It is a particular skill of learning to spot words which aren't vital and not to bother reading them. This will save you time and it will save your eye concentration, but it won't affect your comprehension.

It is a skill that needs practice. It is probably best to practise on less important things than your study, for example a novel when you are on holiday, or the next long memo you get at work…

BPP helps you by emboldening key words in our Study Texts. But before you get over-excited, we certainly wouldn't claim that you can pass the exams by only reading the bold words.

The key words skill

Be discerning in when you apply this skill, however. **Some subjects** (a key example being law, you should think of others) by their nature involve a **need for precision**.

In law an 'and' or an 'or' might be vital.

Recording

(Maximising the effectiveness of your notes)

The notes you have made as you have attended lectures or read through the Study Text relating to a particular subject will form an important part of your learning. Your notes belong to you and to you only.

It doesn't matter what anyone else thinks of them - they are a means to help you understand and remember the subject for your exam. Very few people find pages of A4 densely covered in handwriting easy to read.

We mentioned that design is important when initially taking your notes. As you work through them and come to revise, you may want to rehash your notes again to help you learn from them.

Consider the ideas set out below and on the following page

Cards

BPP produces revision cards called Passcards. These summarise the key points contained within the Study Texts and present them in a visually helpful way.

You may want to rehash your own notes in a similar format, or just use the ones we have put together for you.

Revision cards like this are likely to be useful to linguistic people because they are summarised forms of written notes. However, they are also good for spatial visual people because the notes have been grouped on the cards in a visually helpful way. A bodily kinaesthetic person might find it helpful to produce revision cards because the process of making them (doing it) might help them to remember. The cards present facts in a sensible order for maths logical people.

Personal learning style

How you like your notes to be presented is very much a matter of **personal choice**. This is an area where the **impact of learning styles** can be felt strongly.

Think about it

Think about how you like to be presented with information and adapt your notes to meet this need. We have highlighted what we think matches each learning style, but it is **YOUR learning process, YOU decide…**

I find …

Being a visual person, when I was studying I found poster notes helpful (eg, flow charts showing controls cycles in auditing) which I looked at whenever I went to my fridge, or the front door, or where ever else I had put them.

Maps and posters

BPP uses Big Picture diagrams to illustrate the syllabus. You can produce similar posters to summarise key topics.

These are particularly helpful to **spatial visual** people as they illustrate topics graphically and show the links in a topic. Again, a **bodily kinaesthetic** person may find creating one helpful. If the map uses words rather than pictures, a **linguistic** person may find it useful. As the facts are presented in a logical order again, this method may also help the **maths logical** person.

CDs

BPP produces Success CDs to aid your revision. CDs are likely to help **aural** people.

Musical people might find it helpful to record revision notes set to music and to play them back. Again, the process of making a recording might aid a **bodily kinaesthetic** person. As it is words being recorded, this might also be good for a **linguistic** person.

Videos

You might find it helpful to turn your notes into a video as part of your revision process.

A **bodily kinaesthetic** person may find making a video helpful (they could 'act out' their notes) and a **linguistic** person might find it helpful to speak out and then hear the words in a different way. Again a **musical** person may find it useful to record notes to music.

CD-ROMs and Internet

BPP produces i-L earn and i-Pass CD-ROMs for teaching and for self-assessment. **Maths logical** people benefit from the clear sequencing and structure of the material. **Spatial visual** people may find CD-ROMs visually stimulating. **Bodily kinaesthetic** people may benefit from the 'hands on' interactivity.

Reading and notetaking

Why take notes when reading?

It is **not necessary** to take notes when using a BPP Study Text or i-Learn CD-ROM, because the key details that you need to know are recorded succinctly for you there, and key points are highlighted.

However, **you may want to take notes anyway**. This could be for several reasons:

1. To help you to **concentrate**

2. To note **things which strike you** as you are reading

3. To highlight areas you find **difficult** and **need to verify** with someone

4. As a **review exercise** (see later).

Keep your notes from all papers throughout your studies; when you tackle higher-level papers you will need to remind yourself of what you've already learned.

We discussed taking notes from a lecture on pages 70 to 71. Particularly if you are doing Home Study, you may want to take notes from the reading you do.

Much of what was said in those pages is relevant here. It is important that you take notes that you will want to go back to read; you need to signpost to yourself things which are significant and things which you find difficult.

However, note taking from reading is not an ad hoc exercise. While the words which the lecturer says have a fleeting quality, the words in a book stay there, so you can take your time. Try the following:

Two stage reading process

Skim read the chapter or section you are focusing on in the study session. This involves maximum use of the key word technique and no re-reading paragraphs.

Then conduct a detailed read through, taking notes as you do so.

The skim should make you aware of what the topic is about and what the key issues are, while the detailed read through with note taking helps you to understand the topic.

Use your own words

If you do take notes when reading a book, **you should not just copy out vast chunks** of it. This may aid your memory of what the book says, but does not aid your comprehension of **what it means**.

When trying to learn and understand topics, if you **make notes in your own words** of what you have read, this shows a **comprehension** of the topic. If you can explain it in your own words, **you understand it.** This is an important step in the learning process.

If you understand a topic at the outset, you will find practice and recall becomes substantially easier at the revision stage. **Revision**, after all, is a **reminder of what you know**, not an opportunity to finally understand all that stuff you read a few weeks or months ago!

Approaching texts

At BPP we pride ourselves on producing study materials that include a number of features to help you read our products in the most effective way possible.

1 Introductory pages

NB. The contents page of any book is a useful reference point.

The Introductory pages of a BPP book contain information: about the exam, the contents of the book and also signposts and advice for using the book effectively. In a BPP Study Text, you are likely to find the syllabus and study guide. It is helpful to read this - so that your reading is focused on what you need to know.

2 Introductions and chapter roundups

These are summaries of the chapter, giving you a helpful insight before you dive into the chapter. Knowing in summary what the chapter is about will help your comprehension.

3 Other features

Other features include **use of bold to highlight important words**, shaded boxes for key concepts, use of tables and other visually helpful design features. The books are designed to help reading, by giving your eyes variety and making you aware of the important points.

4 Text order

We have ordered the text in what we see to be a logical way. But you don't have to follow us! Start with a short topic, or one you already know something about - start on page 346 if you want! The chapter introduction should highlight whether you need to be familiar with other topics to understand this one…

5 Text organisation

The way the text is structured shows you the main ideas in each chapter; seeing how the text is organised and the hierarchy of ideas will help you remember the contents better. The chapter title will give you the key subject, the section headers the main themes, and the sub-headers the subsidiary topics.

Reading checklist

▶ Check the syllabus/study guide so that you are clear on what you are aiming to learn
▶ Read the summary of the chapter in the introduction/chapter roundup to get an overview
▶ Take note of key terms and concepts highlighted in the chapter
▶ Re-read the chapter roundup to ensure that you are clear - if not, go back and re-read

Approaching electronic products

Computer-based training

Computer-based training packages such as BPP's i-Learn cover syllabuses on CD-ROM or on-line. They present material in a **visually attractive** way, reinforcing understanding with diagrams, examples and questions. If you have strong **spatial-visual intelligence** you should find them very helpful. As well as using them whilst you're studying a topic, the packages can also be useful for later revision if you've originally used a text. Seeing topics in a different medium can be a big help in reinforcing topics in your memory.

Computer-based assessment

At present computer-based assessment products, such as BPP's i-Pass, mostly consist of **multiple choice and other short answer questions**. They are thus directly relevant to exams that contain these types of question. Some products also show you how to **analyse higher-level scenarios** by asking questions of the material. For all exams these products can be used as a test of knowledge when you've completed a study session or during revision.

CDs

CDs, such as BPP's Success CDs, aim to sum up a syllabus in maybe 90 minutes and provide useful exam tips. They are a method of **m-learning** or mobile learning, as they can be used on the train or the car, or to accompany your early morning gym session. Their focus on key points and exam technique means that if you want to revise a topic, a quick way of doing it at any time will be to listen to the CD session.

Remember at the revision stage you will need to practise exam questions in the way you would answer them in the exam. For many accountancy exams this means answering 20 - 50 mark questions on paper.

On-line tutorials

Many training organisations provide introductory on-line tutorials to each exam, guiding you on **key and difficult areas**, **exam format** and **how to succeed in the exam**. These can be an excellent way of getting into a new topic, and a good reminder at the start of your revision. Some providers also offer tutorials on specific topics, offering a video of the tutor, a menu enabling you to control the delivery, and a window or slides to illustrate what's being said. Unlike a classroom course, you can watch the tutor over and over again in different orders and at different speeds.

Live webcasts

Some training organisations provide live webcasts, where tutors cover the important elements of each section of a syllabus and allow you to **raise questions** that will be answered during the webcast. They may then be archived to allow later viewing.

Discussion forums

Many training organisations run on-line discussion forums enabling students to **exchange views** and **discuss concerns**. They can be particularly useful for helping you understand difficult topics, as other students explain how they grasped them. Discussion forums can be also be good on **practical issues** such as using answer booklets. For case study exams where you need to research an industry, you can use the forums to request or exchange information and to insert web links.

BPP Learning Media and other publishers are developing their range of electronic products. These will certainly play a more and more important part in students' studies, as blended learning approaches evolve.

Following up

It is vital that if you are given information which you do not understand, you seek clarification. You cannot learn accountancy and pass accountancy exams if you do not understand the information that is given to you.

BPP offers a query service to BPP registered students. People who attend classroom courses can always ask their tutors for help. If you are a Home Study student, you will be aware of the email and telephone support systems that BPP offers. Here are some general guidelines:

In class

▶ Try and go with what the lecturer advises (whenever, at the end, etc…)
▶ Remember, if asking during a lecture, it is courteous to raise your hand.

At breaks

▶ If you wait until a break, the lecturer will have more time to answer you. Ask yourself 'is this vital to my understanding of the next two hours?'

Next day

▶ If you were to go home and study a little bit, could you answer your own question? In the long run, the added time spent might pay dividends to your own understanding. You can always ask the next day.

"To ask, or not to ask?
That is the question."

During Home Study

How to ... 📞 Telephone queries

Ringing up a tutor with a query may seem like the easiest thing in the world, but it too can be made more efficient. Here are some guidelines to maximise efficiency:

1 Make a note of your tutor's name so you can ask for them. (Your query may have to be passed to someone else if your tutor is teaching).

2 Make sure you tell them what you are studying (professional scheme, paper, topic) so that they can tune into your need as fast as possible.

3 Be certain you know what your question is (you may find it helpful to write it down first). A tutor wants to help, but won't have time to just chat generally about a topic.

4 Write down the answer you are given. There is no point in making a query and then forgetting what you have been told a minute later.

How to ... ✉ Email queries

The tricks to maximise efficiency in email queries are similar to the telephone ones, particularly steps 2 and 3.

There are some particular benefits to email queries:

1 The key benefit is that **step 4** (write down the answer) is covered automatically. You can keep the email and add it to your notes - but you can't keep a phone call.

2 If you study at night, you can save all your queries to the end of a study session and then email them. You should receive a reply before your next study session.

You may need an immediate answer so the phone is better. But if not, your tutor might find it more convenient to fit answering an email into their timetable, so choosing this option could make queries more efficient for everyone.

Recall

In order to pass exams, you need to be able to recall what you have learnt. Recall is an important aspect of memory.

We are going to look at three areas which it might help you to think about in this area. The three areas are:

▶ Review (review, review, review, review…)

▶ Memory techniques

▶ Practice

We touched on review in Chapter 3, but will revisit it here.

We shall discuss practice briefly in this chapter and will talk more about different kinds of question in Chapter 6.

What's the big deal?

Memory **= Retention + Recall**

Your mind stores a lot more than you might give it credit for. This is the retention aspect of memory. We can see proof of this in the dreams we have. They may seem random sometimes, but often your mind will replay things which have happened or that you have thought of in the day - which you may not have realised that you stored.

> ### I find ...
> That in my first year of accountancy studies, I did a lot of work on introduction to financial decisions late into the evening, because I found it very difficult to understand. I often woke up having dreamed about it - so my mind was obviously taking stuff in, even if I didn't understand it!

Recall is vital to your studies as accountancy is examined - that is, you will have to go into an exam hall and produce what you know on a given day and in answer to given questions. If you have all the knowledge in the world tied up in your brain, but cannot get it out on that given day, you will fail your accountancy exams.

There are **five main factors** to recall:

1	Primacy	These two were covered in Chapter 3, page 64.
2	Recency	
3	Review	Review was also covered briefly in Chapter 3. We look at it in a more practical way on page 83.
4	Linking	We shall consider the implications of 'linking'
5	Standing out	and 'standing out' in memory techniques.

Total recall

What is so great about elephants, anyway? **Your** brain is amazing. It has the capacity to remember everything that your syllabus requires of it.

You need to practise remembering, so that on D Day, you can produce your best.

> I never forget …

Review

Example Day X of lectures

8^{am}

Re-read a **summary** of yesterday's lectures, or jot one down if you did not complete one in the previous day.

9^{am}

Lecture begins. **Take notes** as outlined on page x.

10.30^{am}

At break, get a coffee (of course) but then chat quickly about the lecture with a study partner or friend (ie, swap notes verbally). This establishes whether you are on the same/**right** tracks as one another. (If you are not, ask the tutor who is right.) It also acts as **quick review** of the previous hour and a half.

This step can be repeated three times in the average day of lectures - apply it according to the pattern of yours.

4.30^{pm}

Go home. **Take a break** from your studying for a little while. It is important to clear your head after a day sitting in lectures.

6^{pm}

Work through the **notes** you have taken in the day - **organise** and **re-write** on computer as necessary as previously discussed. This acts as a further review. Then do any **question practice** directed by your tutors.

10^{pm}

Ring mum and see if you can **explain** to her in 15 minutes what you learnt today. Or, if she's not too interested in debits and credits, you could try explaining them to your teddy bear!

We discussed the concept of review in Chapter 3. As we observed there, experts consider that in order to *maximise retention* of information, you should *expose* your brain to the information you want to retain at least *six times*.

As a result of this information, you might want to consider a *study system* such as the one set out on the left hand side of this page. It shows how you can fit at least *four reviews* into a *small period of time*.

There are other ways you can review material; be creative. One example would be compiling a quiz, say 50 questions, focusing on the most important knowledge and techniques in the whole syllabus. Another way is to use a BPP i-Pass CD-ROM to test your knowledge.

You don't have lectures? Try this ● ● ●

The spirit of review as outlined above can also be applied to work you have prepared at home. The two stage reading technique is the first stage - the second read is your first review. Then you can **re-read your notes at the end of each study session and at the beginning of the next one** and on **Saturdays.** And you, too, can chat about accountancy to long-suffering Ted at the end of the day, before giving him a well-earned hug!

Memory techniques

Over the next few pages, we are going to look at two further types of memory techniques. (Remember that the review schedules and study timing tricks that we have already looked at are memory techniques themselves.)

You are probably familiar with the two techniques that we are going to look at. One of them is a technique used in most kinds of learning (even the nursery), the mnemonic, the other is mapping.

A mnemonic is

> **"a pattern of letters or ideas which aids the memory"**

One reason for the popularity of mnemonics is that they can appeal to a large variety of learning styles.

▶ They are comprised of words, so linguistic people are likely to find them helpful.

▶ They can be set to rhymes, so they may appeal to musical people.

▶ As stated above, they follow a pattern, which maths-logical people will like.

▶ They can incorporate a story, which a spatial-visual person may find easy to picture.

Mnemonics are probably the least helpful to a bodily kinaesthetic person but - DON'T STOP READING - the story created may be adapted to a drama, which a bodily kinaesthetic person may find useful.

Mnemonics provide the links which our brain likes to use to recall facts. As you will see on the next page, they can link lists of facts with key words, words to stories and events to rhymes.

Want to know more?

Over the next few pages we will expand on these two techniques, so that we can identify whether you will find it useful to incorporate them into your study systems.

Mnemonics

A key example is the **rhyme**, illustrated below, in the example using the months of the year. The facts which are to be learnt are arranged into a short rhyme. The **metre and rhyme make this easier to remember than a list of facts.**

You may remember this one, too:

In fourteen hundred and ninety-two Columbus sailed the ocean blue.

However, mnemonics do not have to rhyme. They can also consist of **stories**, or a sentence which brings to mind the facts you are trying to remember.

The example below shows the sentence spelling out the first letter of the colours of the rainbow. If you ever learnt music, you may have learnt that

'Every good boy deserves fruit'

to remember which notes fell on lines...

Another type of mnemonic is the **list of words** remembered by being attached to a **key word or acronym**. This is the reverse of the rainbow sentence and it is also illustrated below.

You may have used one to remember financial statement assertions:

Completeness
Occurrence
Valuation
Existence
Disclosure/presentation

...famous **mnemonic stories** are more rare, probably because the memory aide is substantially more useful if the story is relevant to you, but the following story could help you remember the 'i before e' rule:

The school bus always picks me (I) up before Emma, unless Catherine is coming. If she is, the bus goes to Emma's after Catherine's house and picks me up later.

It doesn't have to make sense, so long as you remember it.

You may have found the old rhyme more useful here!

Thirty days hast September,
April, June and November,
All the rest have 31,
Excepting February alone,
For she has 28 days clear
And 29 in each leap year

Richard
Of
York
Gave
Battle
In
Vain

Segregation of duties
Physical
Authorisation and approval
Management

Supervision
Organisation
Arithmetical and accounting
Personnel

The months   The colours of the rainbow   Internal controls

Mnemonics with numbers

$\boxed{\begin{smallmatrix} x & - \\ + & \div \end{smallmatrix}}$ **S**ome people find that it is easy to remember things if they number them.

Illustration

We are going to illustrate remembering with numbers three ways by using the following list of Kings. Some of them have numbers of their own, which may complicate or ease the techniques...we shall see.

William the Conqueror	Richard I
William II	John I
Henry I	Henry III
Stephen and Mathilda	Edward I
Henry II	Edward II

We want to remember all the kings and remember the order in which they reigned, which is the first column followed by the second column.

1. Applying simple numbers

Some people would find that the best way for them to remember that list of kings would be simply to number them in order and then count them off against their fingers.

They would write out the following...

1. William the Conqueror
2. William II
3. Henry I
4. Stephen and Mathilda
5. Henry II
6. Richard I
7. John I
8. Henry III
9. Edward I
10. Edward II

And remember the list by linking the number with the name.

2. Linking the number to the name

If that wasn't you, hopefully you are reading on to discover whether numbers are still for you.

You could link the number with the name to build on the previous technique and remember the list.

For example, using the list to the left, you could remember that William the Conquerer is first (number one) because he was the conqueror and he beat everyone else. William II (2) is then easy to remember, because he follows William 1.

Henry rhymes with three, so you could link those that way. As it is the first time Henry has appeared, it must be Henry I. Using a similar rhyming link, 4 has more, ie more than one person - Stephen and Mathilda.

Perhaps you could use a mathematical idea to link Henry II to Five. Five minus Henry's II is three, which rhymes with Henry.

Are you one of those people?

Can you think of links for the rest of them?

3. The number rhyming technique

The last two 'numbery' memory techniques that we are going to look at may seem a little over complex (you may have thought that number 2 was even taking things a bit far…) but they are effective. I was astonished at the results that I came out with after trying them. But you have to be prepared to go wild with your imagination…

The technique takes the numbers which you have applied to your list of facts to be remembered and links a rhyming word with them which it asks you to picture.

For example:

1	One	Bun
2	Two	Shoe
3	Three	Tree
4	Four	Door
5	Five	Jive
6	Six	Sticks
7	Seven	Heaven
8	Eight	Gate
9	Nine	Dine
10	Ten	Hen

Then you apply the picture to the person you are trying to remember, so for example, you might imagine William the Conqueror having a heavy day in battle and then coming in from the battlefield and having a bun for tea. You might imagine that William II was a tiny man with minuscule feet who had to have his shoes made specially for him, and so on…

Can you think of links between the number images and the rest of the kings?

4. Number pictures, without the rhymes

It may be that you like the idea of technique three, but rhymes are not your thing. The technique is adapted to be more visual than rhyming, as is shown in the next example.

1	One	Spear
2	Two	Swan
3	Three	Bottom
4	Four	
5	Five	
6	Six	
7	Seven	
8	Eight	
9	Nine	
10	Ten	

In this case, the associated word is given to the number because of the way that the number looks. So 1 looks a bit like a spear, 2 looks a bit like a swan and 3 looks like a person's behind, etc…

Now picture these words associated with the people. So, William the Conqueror going into battle with his spear, William II at a great feast eating swan, Henry I with an enormous posterior…

Can you complete the table and link the number images to the kings?

Test it!

Choose your favourite technique and see if you can name the ten kings in the correct order.

Mapping

Mapping is another very visual technique which correlates to both the 'linking' and 'standing out' aspects of our memory.

The technique of 'mapping' has various different titles. It is sometimes called mindmapping, or drawing a mindmap, or can be called making a spider-diagram. We have touched on the technique on page 75, as a possible way to build up your notes.

Here we will look at how you create a 'map' and what the benefits of such a map are for your recall.

Key points

A mind map is supposed to sum up a lot of information, indeed whole topics, in a relatively small space. It involves you identifying 'tags' (these can be words, pictures or symbols) which will trigger your memory on a particular topic.

Commonly, mindmaps will grow from a central point, but this does not have to be the case. The mindmap might be showing a certain process, so it might grow in a linear fashion. It could be illustrating a concept which builds on itself, and grows more like a tree.

Some examples of mindmaps are set out on the next few pages. Looking at these is probably the best way to familiarise yourself with the topic - but do not assume that this is the only way to create mindmaps.

Think of a mindmap as being a graphical representation of your thoughts on a subject - and ensure that the finished product reflects the way you perceive what it is that you are trying to remember.

Express yourself

Do not time yourself when it comes to mindmaps. Consider use of **colour**, **typefaces**, **letter case**, **arrows** . . . whatever helps you remember and makes things STAND OUT. Go for it . . .

The elephant mindmap

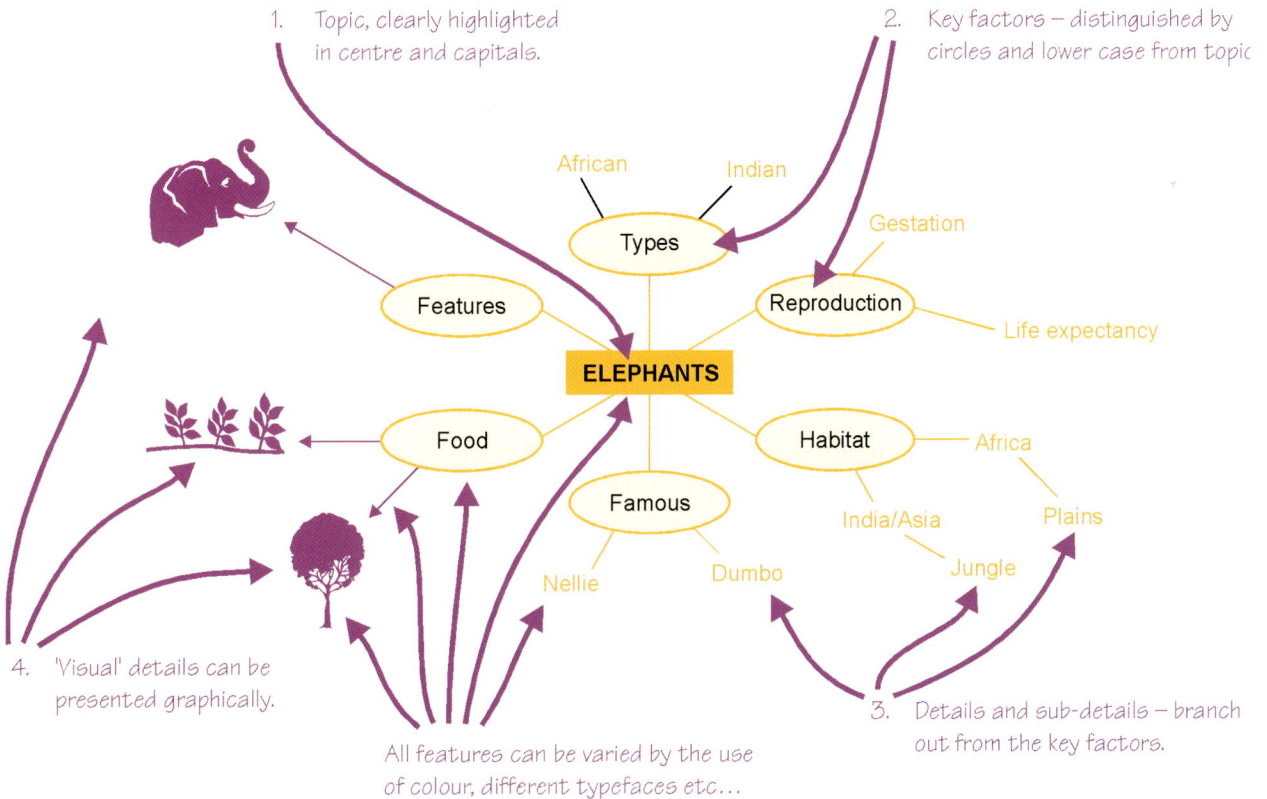

1. Topic, clearly highlighted in centre and capitals.

2. Key factors – distinguished by circles and lower case from topic

African   Indian

Types

Gestation

Reproduction

Life expectancy

Features

ELEPHANTS

Food

Habitat   Africa

Famous

India/Asia   Plains

Nellie   Dumbo   Jungle

4. 'Visual' details can be presented graphically.

All features can be varied by the use of colour, different typefaces etc…

3. Details and sub-details – branch out from the key factors.

---

1   This mindmap grows from a central point.

2   Key factors pan out like spokes from the central point, showing the important things to remember.

3   Details relating to each key factor branch out of those circles.

4   Symbols or pictures can be used to summarise details.

On the following pages, some more examples are given for you to look at.

The Olympic mindmap

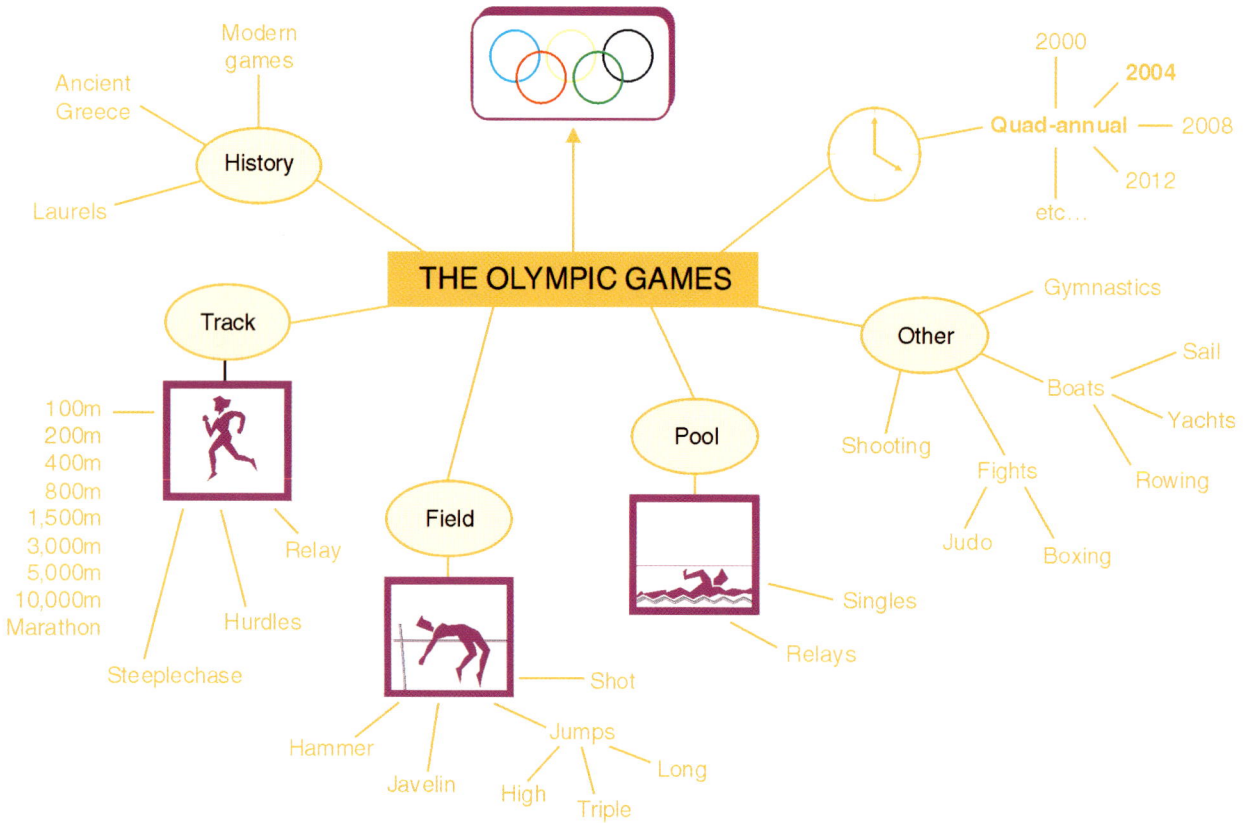

The Olympic mindmap centred on "THE OLYMPIC GAMES" with branches:

- **History**: Modern games, Ancient Greece, Laurels
- **Track**: 100m, 200m, 400m, 800m, 1,500m, 3,000m, 5,000m, 10,000m, Marathon, Relay, Hurdles, Steeplechase
- **Field**: Shot, Jumps (Long, High, Triple), Javelin, Hammer
- **Pool**: Singles, Relays
- **Other**: Gymnastics, Boats (Sail, Yachts, Rowing), Fights (Judo, Boxing), Shooting
- **Quad-annual**: 2000, 2004, 2008, 2012, etc...

Analysis

This mindmap also grows from a central point, with key factors ranged around it. It uses a combination of words and symbols to jog the memory. Details to be remembered branch out from the key points, and **sub-points** branch out from those details.

The study process mindmap

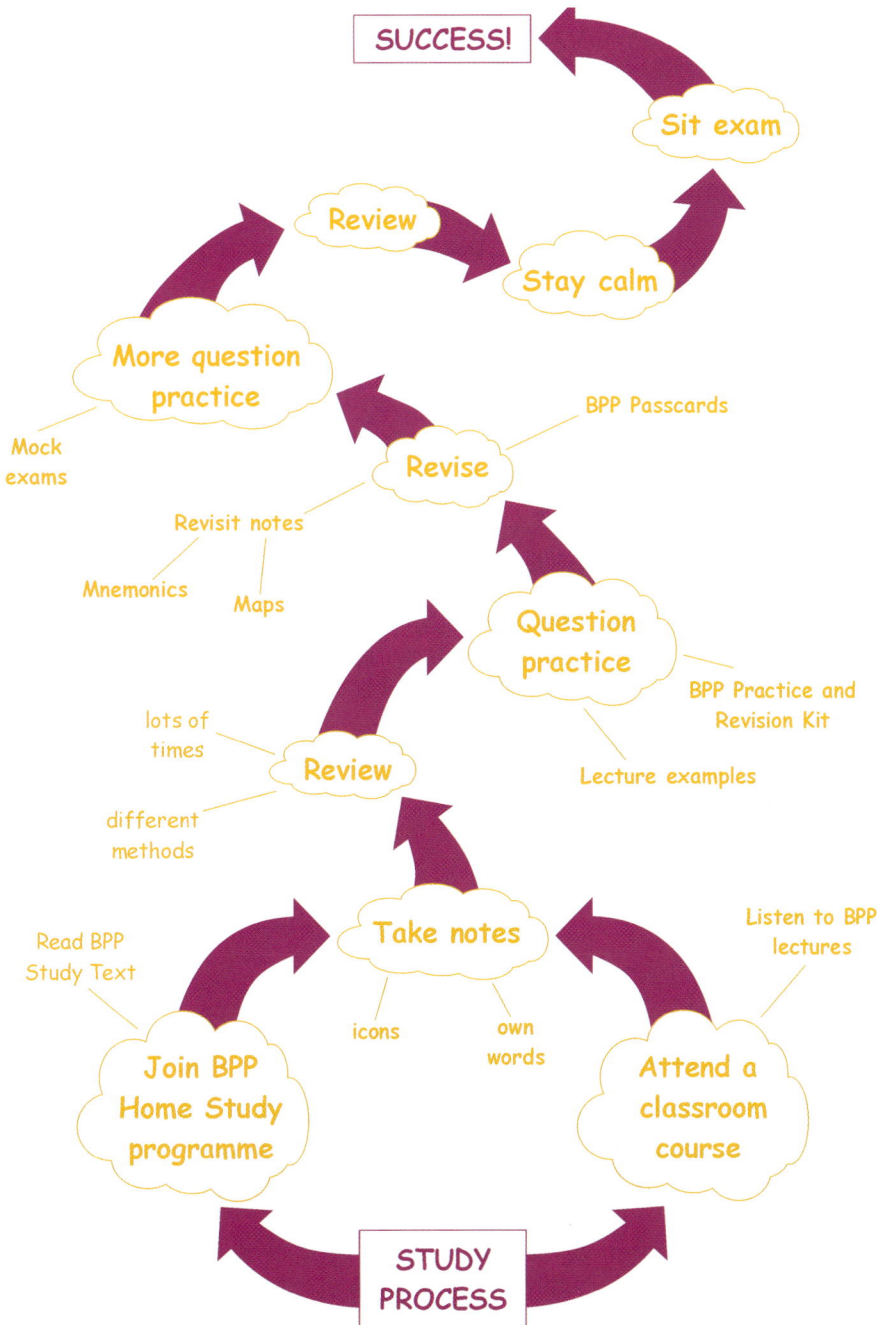

SUCCESS!

Sit exam

Review

Stay calm

More question practice

Mock exams

Revisit notes

Mnemonics

Maps

Revise

BPP Passcards

Question practice

lots of times

Review

different methods

BPP Practice and Revision Kit

Lecture examples

Read BPP Study Text

Take notes

Listen to BPP lectures

icons

own words

Join BPP Home Study programme

Attend a classroom course

STUDY PROCESS

Analysis

The mindmap to the left is linear, rather than round because it shows a process. The key stages of the study process are shown in cloud shapes to highlight them. Sub-elements are shown branching off. The large coloured arrows show a clear path through the process.

'Success' is shown at the top as the summit of our endeavour and what we are aiming at. The mindmap on the left stems from the central point and is more comprehensive in the detail included, showing how you can vary the detail on the mindmap according to its purpose.

Developing business awareness

Links with study material

Look out for links in the business pages to your study material; how might the management theories that you've studied help the businesses generate strategies, how might financial analysis such as breakeven calculations aid decision making.

The real world

Many students struggle in Final level exams because they can't answer questions in the context of the actual world of business; they can regurgitate the textbook or e-learning material they've used, but don't have much idea of how what they've learnt works in practice. When they do quote examples, these are often examples that aren't relevant to the situation in the question.

If you read the business press regularly you can significantly improve your chances of passing, particularly in exams testing business and financial strategy.

The stories you read can:

▶ **Supplement what your texts and e-learning material say** and show you what factors are most important in business decision-making

▶ Help develop your **analysis skills**

▶ Provide **relevant examples** that aren't the same boring ones quoted in hundreds of scripts

A good way of approaching an article is to look at a headline and consider the issue(s) it raises; then instead of reading the full article straightaway, creating a list of questions that are suggested by the headline. Then read the article to see how many of your questions are answered. This will develop your ability to generate ideas when you read exam scenarios.

Questioning business decisions

▶ What are the reasons behind the decision?
▶ What impacts will the decision have?
▶ How will the course of action chosen be financed?

Retaining business stories

You can obviously take cuttings from newspapers and magazines, or copy and save articles from the Internet. However it's better to treat the articles as you would a textbook and only retain a digest of the main points.

Summarising stories will mean not only that you have a more manageable store of material, but summarising the content will help fix it more in your mind. By summarising you will develop the skill of determining the importance of the data you're given; this will help you analyse business scenarios in the exam.

Practising summarising articles of different length will also help you cope with different sorts of scenario in the exam.

Writing a full paragraph rather than notes of the main points will also help develop your writing skills.

What to read

The Financial Times and Economist are very good sources of stories, but reading the business pages of any quality newspaper will be helpful. Many Sunday papers have summaries of the week's main business stories.

> Using the Internet to read international stories on the websites of foreign publications can help develop your insight into global issues.

▶ How will stakeholders (interested parties) react?
▶ How will the company's competitive position be affected?
▶ What will the company have to do to implement the decision successfully?

Skills developed by question practice

Interpretation of question requirements

Question requirements indicate how much depth and breadth your answer should have, and the style and format you should use. You also will learn the clues given in questions that will determine your approach.

Choosing the right content

Practice will help you understand the right mix of content for your answer. This includes how much theory to include, also how to use factual detail and practical examples to support your answer. You also may see that stating the obvious may gain you marks.

Answer structuring

Structuring your answer poorly may hide the knowledge you have. Question practice shows you how answers should be structured, the right order of points, and how points need to be developed. It's particularly important to plan a good structure and stick to it if you're answering an exam on paper, as you won't have computer cut and paste facilities available if you do change your mind while answering.

Managing your time

The time available to you and the marker is a limited resource. Practice shows you how much you can write in the time; it brings home the importance of allocating your time and prioritising the most important points so that you develop them properly. Practice also makes you think about making your answer easy to mark.

Get your answers marked

For **higher level papers** in particular, you cannot afford to leave question practice until just before the exam. Because it may not be easy to determine how good your answer is, you should ideally have your answers **marked** by a **knowledgeable person**, a tutor or someone doing the course with you. The marker's assessment may highlight points that are not obvious to you, such as a lack of business awareness or over-complex language. You can then work on these skills. Even if you are marking your own answers, **be critical**. Ask yourself **why** you are awarding yourself marks before giving yourself a pass.

Different types of subject ...

Financial Accounting is largely a practical subject.

You will have to:

1 Understand

2 **Do**

> This is likely to be good news for **bodily kinaesthetic** people

In the exam, you are likely to have requirements like 'Prepare a cash flow statement in accordance with FRS 1' or 'Produce the consolidated cash flow statement'. This means that practising doing these things is essential.

Law is a theoretical subject.

You will have to:

1 Understand

2 **Explain** or **Apply**

> This is likely to be good news for **maths logical** people

In the exam you are likely to be given a scenario and asked 'What is X's legal position?' This means that practising to think through a situation logically, applying legal rules is vital.

> *In Chapter 2, we outlined the various types of subject that you will be studying.*
>
> *The subjects are very different, and it makes sense that you should not approach them all in the same way, to achieve the best that you can in each of them.*
>
> *You may already be able to suggest or guess which subjects you will find most easy to handle.*
>
> *However, if you find out all you can about the nature of each subject, you should be able to tailor your approach in the best way. This may mean practising study skills that don't come naturally to you.*

Sherlock

Basically we are suggesting that a **key study skill** is the power to investigate how to approach the subject, before you dive in ...

You can do this by asking someone who knows or by reading the introduction or introductory chapter of your Study Text.

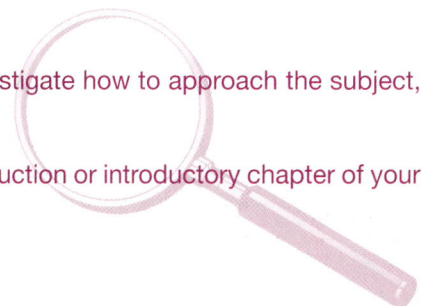

Deciding whether to take exams on computer

Foundation exams

The main advantage with taking these exams on computer is convenience. You are not limited to sitting exams twice a year; exam centres offer much more frequent exam sessions. You will not have to wait six months for a resit if you fail. Computer exams allow you to receive your results immediately after you've finished the exam and provide feedback showing where you've gone wrong. Some tuition providers offer integrated courses for computer-based exams rather than separate teaching and revision courses, reducing the study leave you need.

There are some features of computer-based Foundation exams that students dislike. Being in a computer room where everyone is typing away on the computer can be noisier than sitting in a much bigger exam hall where students are taking a paper-based exam. The clock ticking exam time away at the corner of the computer screen can be a distraction and an incitement to panic. Also you can't glance through the whole computer exam quickly, so until you've gone through all the questions you can't determine which ones are the most difficult.

Higher level exams

Being able to use a computer for a higher level exam can mean that your answers are better presented. Markers won't have to read your handwriting and it's easier to add headings and shorten paragraph length. Spreadsheets allow routine calculations to be done quickly, allowing more time to cope with the exam's more demanding requirements. (And if, as is likely, you use a keyboard a lot at work, you should find using a computer in the exam even more advantageous.)

If however you sit your last exam on computer having taken most other exams on paper, you will find sitting at the keyboard different and possibly disruptive to your exam routine. Using exam software that differs from the software you'd normally use can also cause problems. In particular some exam software doesn't highlight spelling and grammatical errors, and if you normally type quickly you may rely on these features to identify mistakes.

Ultimately your choice may be determined by how near you are to an exam centre offering computer-based exams.

Learning
styles

Types of
subject

Study
environment

Study
skills

Revision

Types of
question

Exam
paper

An
assortment

Revision

The last few weeks

This chapter is about the period leading up to your exams and how you should approach revision.

What not to do

If you just set out with the intention of 'revising everything before the exam':

▶ Your revision will be superficial; you will not have spent enough time revising actively, **or**

▶ You will run out of time, and find that you have not covered important topics

Your time is a limited resource. You must approach revision methodically. Organising your revision involves taking certain key decisions.

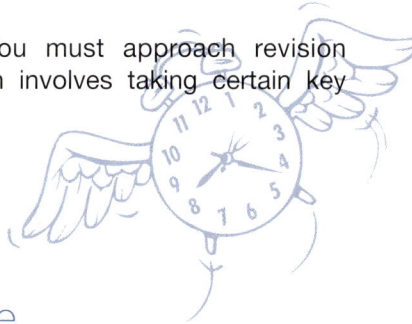

What to revise

When to revise

How to revise

Timetable

Remember the revision timetables that you have used for school or university exams in the past and jot down an example. If you have never prepared a revision timetable before, try now to think about what it should contain.

When

Overall timetable

At the start of your revision period, you should draw up an overall timetable to make sure you cover everything you need to cover in every paper.

You also should give thought to:

▶ *Order. You may wish to tackle the most important topics first.*

▶ *Skills. You need to practice key skills (analysis, communication).*

▶ *Revision course. Your timetable should fit around what you are doing on the course.*

▶ *Final stages. You should allow time at the end to sit mock exams and re-read passcards.*

Daily timetables

Having completed an overall timetable, you should draw up weekly and daily timetables. You should avoid falling far behind your overall timetable; however you should build in flexibility if certain topics need more revision than first planned.

Our timetable

Our revision timetable has the following features.

1 Time
The timings depend on you; you may start with an hour's revision before breakfast or finishing the day by tackling a full exam question from the kit.

2 Subjects
Revising different subjects during the day can keep you mentally fresh. In our timetable law revision after lunch contrasts with spending the rest of the day on financial accounting.

3 Comments
Writing down why you're revising a subject forces you to think about what aspects are the most important.

4 Method
Full exam questions are alternated with shorter exercises focusing on knowledge and question approach.

5 Points forward
These are points you would incorporate into your timetables for future days.

6 Breaks
Breaks are marked for coffee, tea, lunch and dog walking.

Having talked about how you should divide your time up, we are going to move on to consider which subjects you should spend the **most time** revising.

Revision timetable - Saturday 11 June

Time	Subject	Comments	Method	Pts forward
9.00	Statement of Principles	Possible question on basic principles	Read chapter summary/passcard List main principles without notes Read article in April's student magazine	Attempt part question in 3 days time
10.00	Coffee			
10.15 Coffee 11.15 - 11.30	Group accounts	Certain compulsory question per examiner guidance	Questions 39, 42 revision kit - full questions	Ran out of time; accounting for minority interests problems Consult tutor Do another question
12.30	Lunch			
1.30	Unfair dismissal	Certain MCQ/ Probable optional question	Chapter 10 text quick quiz Q63 revision kit- answer plan	Satisfactory. Read passcard and listen to success tape in days before exam
2.30	Tea			
2.45	Cash flow statement	Possible compulsory question, full single company CFS	Q65 revision kit - full question	Included non-cash expenses, test self on common non-cash expenses (Text p100) on Friday
3.45	Tea			
4.00	Statutory accounts proformas	Likely compulsory question; missed out elements of profit and loss a/c previously	Write out proformas Attempt i-Pass questions	100% correct; try again in a week's time.
5.00	Walk dog			

Evening sessions

Much of your revision may be done in the evenings. Most of the points we make opposite apply to evening revision as well, particularly revising different subjects in different ways and taking short breaks between each session.

What (1)?

Don't forget...

Often students forget to revise certain essentials that are vital when answering exam questions:

Key terms

Report formats

Computation layouts and proformas

Basic principles

Strengths

Even if you feel happy with a topic, you must test yourself to see if you are as good at it as you think you are.

A lot of learning can be a dangerous thing

For higher level papers, it's easy to spend too much time revising basic factual knowledge, cluttering your mind with excessive detail. You should spend most time practising questions; the facts you learn should be those you are most likely to use to support your analysis or argument.

Key topics

At the start of your revision you should draw up a list of the key topics for each paper. You can identify the important topics in various ways.

▶ Recur regularly on the paper·

▶ Underlie whole paper (e.g. qualities of information)

▶ Often the subject of compulsory questions

▶ Current issues

▶ Subject of recent articles by examiner

▶ Shown as high priority in text/home study material

▶ Key * points made by lecturer

▶ Tutor tips

These are the areas where you should spend most time, topics on which you need to practise full questions. Remember to cover all examinable aspects of a topic; for example as well as revising a technique, don't forget to revise the weaknesses of that technique.

Be careful…

of over-revising, spending too much time on a topic or getting bogged down in a small area of the syllabus. You can avoid this by assessing what is the maximum that a question about the topic would ask.

Tips

Treat tips with caution. Some tutors will tip all significant topics; others will hedge their tips with considerable reservations.

It's important to understand **why** a subject has been tipped. A tip on the basis that the examiner has written a recent article stressing the topic's importance is stronger than a tip that the subject has not been examined for three years 'and is bound to come up sooner or later.'

What (2)?

Difficult areas

Hopefully some topics you found difficult to start with will seem easier when you come to revise them. However there may be some areas where you still lack confidence.

▶ You just 'don't like' the area; you find it dull or can't see the point of it.

▶ You highlighted the subject as a difficult (!) subject when taking notes.

▶ You noted problems when you answered questions or when you reviewed the material.

Having identified problem areas, you need to decide what to do about them. We make some suggestions opposite and will discuss how to revise actively later in this chapter.

Stay positive

Don't get depressed that you have identified an area as difficult; remember instead that you are doing something about it. Other students will have found the same topic difficult and given up.

Don't get bogged down

You should also focus on what is most important about the area, what is likely to earn you the most marks. Don't spend a lot of time trying to understand a complication which will only be worth two marks at maximum in the exam.

Lack of knowledge

If your problem is a failure of knowledge, concentrate on methods that test knowledge such as writing out summaries, quick quizzes and MCQs

Computations

If you struggle with computations, go back to the examples in the text, noting the logic behind each stage. Then practise a question from the kit, referring back to the text if you struggle. Having noted your problems, do a second question without referring to the text, and assess why your performance has differed from the question where you did refer to the text.

Higher skills

If you've had problems with questions involving higher level skills, full question practice will give you more confidence in applying those skills. Write down as part of your plan your previous weaknesses and whilst you're answering the question, constantly remind yourself of them - are you saying enough about why the figures in the accounts have changed? Are your recommendations clear and specific?

Do ask!

Above all don't be afraid to seek help. Maybe someone you know had similar difficulties, was able to overcome them and can help you deal with the problems.

What? (3)

And the rest?

We have discussed how you select areas which need a lot of attention when you revise.

However...

You also need to consider whether your revision has sufficient breadth, whether you are revising enough subjects.

Breadth of revision is particularly important on certain types of paper.

▶ Many lower level exams consist partly or wholly of compulsory MCQs/short answer questions which cover all major areas of the syllabus.

▶ With higher level papers containing a mixture of compulsory and optional questions, the topics covered by compulsory questions may be unpredictable.

One check that you can use is to look over exam papers for the last few years in your revision kit. You can check that following your revision plan would have enabled you to answer all of the compulsory questions and sufficient optional questions on each paper.

Remember however that although you need to cover a good breadth of subjects, you should not spend equal time on each.

Past problems and question spotting

Old examiner's reports can provide clues on areas that many candidates did not revise at all. These areas are **very tempting** for examiners.

Remember also that many examiners try to catch out students who limit their revision to the topics they think will be examined. The examiners may set the same topic in two sittings in a row, or include in the compulsory section of the exam a topic that has previously only appeared in the optional section.

How?

Look at the definitions of revising given below. Some key words have been emboldened. These key words are going to point us in the direction of how we should revise.

A Verb

Remember when you were in Primary school and you were first taught all this stuff? What is verb? - a **DOING** word.

You must be **active** in your revision.

B Examine

Revision is not a process of casting an eye over things - rather a process of looking **carefully**. The examiner is going to examine what you know - **you** need to **get in first**.

C Reconsider

Think things through again. At the end of the course, you will be able to **see links** and connections and it will all begin to make sense as a **coherent** body of information.

D Improve one's knowledge

Remember, revision is an **enhancing process**. We are going to take what you have learnt and make it exam sized and shaped.

E Re-read/look at again

As you will see in the next few pages, we do not want you just to read - but you must be sure that in your revision phase it is **genuinely second time** around. If there are areas you have not covered - cover them before you start.

One thing that has been emphasised in this book so far is the need for you to be proactive in your approach to study.

When it comes to revision, we still want you to be proactive, but we also want you to get interactive. Passive revision is not going to be effective.

How you revise is really up to you. You are likely to have done it before, so you probably have some tried and tested methods.

But read through the next few pages, so that you can be critical about your methods, and perhaps enhance your skills.

It can be helpful as you approach the exam to change your learning environment to what you'll encounter in the exam room, sitting on an upright chair at a small, uncluttered table.

To revise

A **Verb.** 1. **B** **Examine** and improve or amend, **C** **reconsider** and alter

A **Verb.** 2. **E** **Reread work done previously** to **D** **improve one's knowledge,** typically for an examination

It derives from the French **E** 'to **look at again**'.

Revision pie chart

To the right is a very simple pie chart showing four stages of revision.

Once you have achieved your planning and know *what* you want to revise and *when* you are going to do it, you need to know *how to...*

You may have methods which work well for you, but you might want to consider the *reasons* behind the four stage plan, and assess whether you want to incorporate the four stage plan into your personal revision methods.

Many of the techniques used are going to be microcosms of the study skills set out in Chapter 4.

Remember also not to spend most of your time reading and writing: teaching and doing questions test your knowledge and understanding are sufficient.

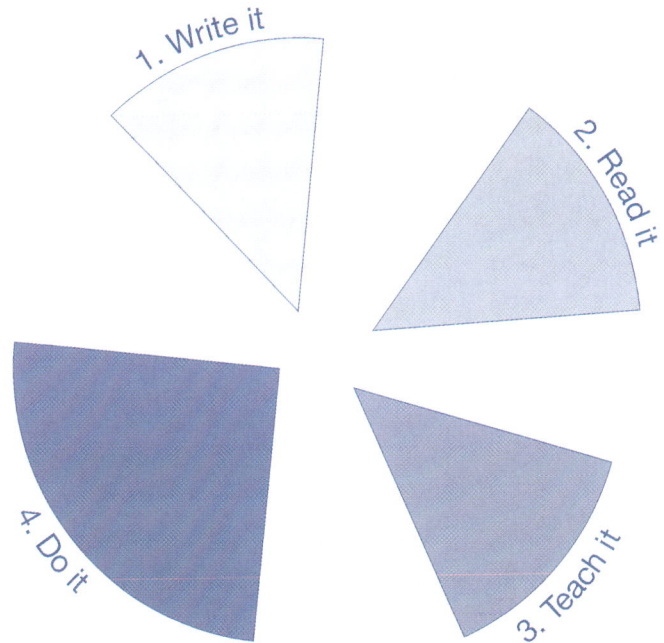

1. Write it

2. Read it

3. Teach it

4. Do it

Four step revision programme

In the next pages we are going to point out some **benefits** of each of the four stages and also look at some tips and ideas for **how** to carry out each stage.

Write it!

Tips

1 The revision notes do not have to be predominantly in words - although this will partly be driven by the topics you are revising.

2 Many people find that transferring their notes onto A5 cards is a useful exercise - the cards are manageable and more user friendly than big A4 sheets.

3 Visual people may find that they can visualise particular revision cards - particularly if they have designed the cards to assist that process:

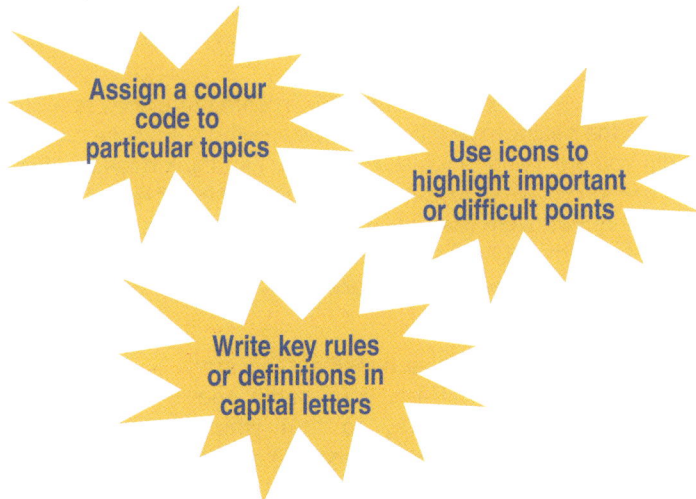

Assign a colour code to particular topics

Use icons to highlight important or difficult points

Write key rules or definitions in capital letters

Passcards

BPP have completed step 1 for you, if you are short of time or paper…

Our handy pocket-sized passcards contain exam focused revision materials with topics summarised for you in bite-sized chunks.

Read it!

Why?

Do you remember what we said about review? You should review material several times over to aid the memorising process.

Once you have created notes, the only way to review whilst actually using them is to read them.

If your notes have been made in the form of posters or flowcharts, then 'read' might in this instance mean 'look at'.

Tips

1 Read actively. This may mean reading out loud, or reading back and forth, flipping over pages, testing yourself.

2 On a similar theme, while you read the notes which you have prepared for yourself, make use of other resources available to you - quickly go through the i-learn CD-ROM, use the quick quizzes given in the Study Text, for example, to test your memory of what you are reading, while you are reading it.

3 See if place association helps your revision:

Read through different sets of notes in different places, the bus, the library, the beach - see if you can build memory associations with the facts you are trying to remember. If you can think back to where you were when you were reading, your mind may find it easier to recall the facts that you were reading. Alternatively, if you use posters, where you put them will help to create a link - double entries for stock on the fridge, cash flow proforma above my bed, etc…

4 If you don't like reading, and feel that this stage is impossible - vary your review method. Tape your notes and then listen to them actively, in a similar way to that which is outlined above. Alternatively use the BPP Success CD that covers your exam.

2 for the price of 1

While revising, try **reading out loud,** even if it is not your usual custom. That way, you'll be **reading it,** and receiving the benefit of **hearing it,** too.

The review phase

You should try to vary this phase as much as you can - your mind likes things to be distinctive, and as you cannot vary what you are learning beyond the call of the syllabus, varying your method of review should add this element of distinction.

Teach it!

Tips

1 If you have kind people who are willing to help you in this situation, you should vary to whom you explain all the facets of your financial management course - even the best of friends can be put off by sustained exposure to technical detail!

2 Alternatively, you could genuinely use your cat or your ted - while a real person may be able to challenge your understanding, in reality, they are probably not likely to, so it doesn't matter whether your pupil is animate or not!

3 If you can carry out this phase with someone who is able to challenge your understanding - a study buddy perhaps? - so much the better. Become debating partners and you will be better equipped to approach the examiner's challenges. You could also set each other quizzes on key topics and mark each other's question practice.

Communcation, Communcation, **Communcation**

Teaching others is a good way of **practising the skill of communicating your understanding**, which is a **vital link** in the exam chain. In some exams, such as the Case Study, there will be marks specifically available for communication skills; however in all exams with longer questions your ability to communicate will be one of the factors underlying the marks you score.

Do it!

Why?

*We have already noted the importance of doing **question practice** as part of the learning process.*

*At the revision stage, bear in mind that the **reason** you are learning all these facts is **to answer questions** in the exam, question practice tests the knowledge and skills you'll need.*

*Practising questions will also help you practise important things such as exam **technique** (in relation to timing and such like) and **discipline** in your answers, which, examiners comment time and time again, can make or break a candidate's script.*

*Another facet of 'do it!' is this: **if your paper is relevant** to a department that you work in, **use your work as an act of revision**. Consciously talk yourself through what you are doing and why.*

Tips

1 As part of your revision planning, you should timetable time to do questions in full. You'll find it helpful to attempt questions from the start of your revision to highlight where you're strong and where you need to do more work.

2 Identify questions which you want to tackle at each stage of your revision, and then tick them off when they are done. Note down mistakes you make or key points in the answer guidance; try to learn at least one thing from each question you do.

3 At the revision phase, you should only really be attempting questions that are exam standard, unless you are still finding an area particularly hard.

4 As we said earlier, if you are running out of time in your revision phase, it is still worth using questions as part of your revision. If you do not have time to complete a full answer, try:

▶ Doing an answer plan instead of a full answer.
▶ Attempting parts of a calculation

5 If you are taking exams on computer you should be practising questions using the technology that you will use in the actual exam. You must attempt any on-line demos provided by the examining bodies.

Question practice

BPP's Practice & Revision Kits contain lots of helpful **guidance** about questions - which to tackle and in what order. They highlight key questions, explaining **why** you should do them, and contain a question plan. You will find this helpful when it comes to question practice in your revision.

Remember also the kits also contain at least one mock exam. You should ensure that towards the end of your revision you attempt one or more mock exams in as near as full exam conditions as you can get, so that you are thoroughly practised and develop a **routine** for tackling exams.

Know your exam

As part of your revision, you should make sure that you are aware of what the syllabus contains and what has happened in recent exams. This questionnaire indicates what you should find out.
You should complete the General section at the start of your revision. You can also complete the Last three exams section then; however if you are taking any of the last three exams as full mock exams you should postpone answering the questions for that paper until after you have taken it.

General

▶ What are the major headings in the syllabus?

▶ Has the examiner provided any guidance on the format questions will take or his or her preferences on ways questions should be answered?

▶ Has the examiner written any articles on this paper? Have you read them?

Last three exams

▶ Did any topics appear in all of the last three exams?

▶ Have you looked at the mark schemes published by the examining body?

▶ How many marks were available in the last three exams for calculations?

▶ How many marks were available in the last three exams for written discussion?

▶ What do the mark schemes tell you about how calculations are marked?

▶ What do mark schemes tell you about how written discussions are marked?

▶ What were the five most serious weaknesses identified in the last three examiner's reports (use your judgement if the examiner identified more than five)?

▶ Could you have answered all parts of all the compulsory questions in the last three exams?

▶ Could you have answered all parts of all the optional questions in the last three exams? If not, could you have answered enough optional questions?

▶ Were any significant topics not examined in any of the last three exams? [This is not an encouragement to question spot; don't be surprised if they are not tested in your exam. However, examiners for most papers have to cover all syllabus areas over a certain length of time.]

Did you accept the challenge earlier in the chapter to list ways you can revise a topic quickly?

Here are our suggestions.

1 Read and summarise the chapter roundups and BPP passcards

To make sure you have taken in what you've read, try to **list** the ten **most important facts** or areas about the subject, or draft a quick **mindmap**.

2 Do the quick quiz

You can use the **quick quiz** to **identify gaps** in your knowledge where you need to refresh your memory. You may well find that removing these gaps pays dividends in the exam.

3 Do the MCQs

For papers containing MCQs, doing the MCQs **early** in your revision of an area can direct your attention to certain vital topics; you may have **struggled** with some of the MCQs or there may be facts and techniques that are tested as MCQs **over and over again**. BPP Kits and i-Pass CD-ROMs provide lots of MCQs for practice.

4 Audit the answer

WARNING! Auditing the answer can give **false reassurance**. Your belief that you would have come up with all the points that the answer contains may well be **false**. Nevertheless auditing the answer can provide some value, if you understand the **approach** the answer has taken. Also have a look at the **examiner's comments**, and think how you can ensure that you won't make the mistakes the examiner highlights. Lastly **don't** learn the answer, expecting to be able just to reproduce it in your exam. Even in lower level papers, examiners will never set questions that are identical to past questions.

5 Do an answer plan and/or attempt parts of the calculation

Going some way to **answer the question** is more valuable than just auditing the answer. Your brain will be more receptive to what the answer says if you have already spent a few minutes thinking about what you should do. You will also be **testing key skills**, tackling computations or structuring an answer.

Living through revision

Diet

Most importantly, remember to eat at all! Then remember to eat well - not quick snacks, but proper meals.

Sleep

It is vital that you sleep properly through your revision period so that your brain is rested. If you are having trouble sleeping, avoid working late into the night and try traditional methods, such as a glass of hot milk before you go to bed.

Enjoy yourself!

Lastly, enjoy yourself! We have highlighted the importance of taking time off. If you are taking time off, but spending that time thinking about the work that is sitting on your desk, then the time off is not worth anything. **If you take the time, really take it off!**

You may find that you experience the **association** phenomenon again - 'I remember revising all about the Stock Exchange in the morning on that day we went to Alton Towers in the afternoon…'

Learning
styles

Types of
subject

Study
environment

Study
skills

Revision

Types of
question

Exam
paper

An
assortment

Types of
question

Introduction

Content

Questions in exams take many different forms, and require answers ranging from a single letter, word or figure to a report requiring several hours to write.

However the main steps to follow are the same whatever the question. We explain what these stages are on these two pages, and go on to discuss in detail how to approach each type of question.

Remember!

Failure to answer the question set contributes to more exam failures than any other reason.

Remember!

The marks available for the question should determine the time you spend on it.

Focus on the requirements

The first step is to read and analyse the requirements of the question.

1 Instructions

The instructions will indicate whether the question is testing knowledge and understanding (describe), application (calculate), or analysis and evaluation (discuss, recommend).

2 Purpose

The purpose will determine the information you bring in and the techniques you should use. The recipient of your answer will be important in determining its purpose.

3 Scope

You need to identify specifically which aspect(s) of which subject area(s) are being examined.

Analyse the details

What you are looking for is the key information that will show you how to apply the question requirements and that you will use in your answer. This may include your role, business details and who will be reading your answer. Analyse actively; jot down ideas, mark the question paper with notes of what you should do or in which part of the question you should use the information, also link related points together.

Some features recur regularly in certain types of questions. Question practice will enable you to spot these, and also help you identify traps set to distract you.

"Students are advised to focus on core topics of the syllabus and to practise past examination questions to ensure that they have an adequate grasp of the topics." *An examiner*

Which subject is the examiner talking about?

118

Plan your answer

Planning does not just involve writing down all the points you think you can make. It involves consideration of which points are the most important, also

▶ The structure of your answer: which points in which order
▶ The format of your answer
▶ The timing, how long each section of your answer should take and leaving time at the end to finish off

Check before you start that your plan makes sense. Confirm that your plan covers all relevant points and does not include irrelevancies.

Write your answer

Try to obtain all the easy marks you can before you move onto the difficult parts of a question. You may earn easy marks by giving a definition, writing out a proforma or slotting information from the question straight into your answer.

You can put a favourable slant on your answer by using clear English, short paragraphs, and underlined headings. While you're writing ask yourself regularly whether what you're writing is relevant. Using the question requirements and scenario details as headings can help to demonstrate your answer's relevance.

Finish off

You can gain crucial marks by finishing off and tidying up your work.

▶ Total your calculations
▶ Draw conclusions or make recommendations
▶ Link main answer to appendices/workings
▶ Improve presentation (extra underlinings)

Features of a well-planned answer

▶ **Focused on key issues**

▶ **Good breadth**

▶ **Good depth**

▶ **Well-structured**

▶ **Points linked clearly**

▶ **Tidy presentation**

Writing your answer is much easier if you do a good plan.

The quote comes from the examiner's report for the CAT Paper Managing Finances.

Unless you are a very well-read CAT student, you are unlikely to have answered correctly; examiners for all types of subject have expressed the same sentiments.

Multiple choice questions (MCQs)

Focus on the requirements

If you are doing your exam on paper (as opposed to on computer) you may prefer to read through all the questions first. You will then be able to see which questions you can answer easily, and which questions seem more difficult or will take longer to answer.

Generally question instructions will be straightforward, for example 'answer all the questions in Part A.'

The requirements will also contain instructions about how you should give your answer and what you should do if you change your mind. You should read these carefully; any answers that are ambiguous will be marked wrong.

Analyse the details

Although some MCQs will be straightforward, others may contain traps or irrelevant information.

You may find that some of a wording in a question seems familiar. If you think that you recognise it, you should nevertheless read the requirement and options carefully; do not assume the question is identical to one you have encountered before.

A warning

Time management is as important in tackling MCQs and other OTs as it is for more traditional questions. It's therefore useful to practise MCQs in groups, so that you experience tackling a number of MCQs within a time limit.

Which one of the following is not a false statement?

A   Charles Dickens was not an English novelist.

B   Two plus two is not five.

C   The Beatles came from New York.

D   Peru, Bolivia, Paraguay and Tunisia are all countries in South America.

Plan your answer

Timing is an important decision; you need to decide how long on average you can allocate to each MCQ.

Even if MCQs represent x% of the marks, that does not always mean you should spend x% of the available time on them. Examiners sometimes expect that MCQs will be completed in a shorter time than suggested by their mark allocation.

Write your answer

Even if one of the options matches your own answer, be careful; the incorrect answers (distracters) are usually answers involving traps or common errors. You should make sure you take all relevant details into account and work through every stage of calculations. Workings will help you answer questions methodically, even if you don't get any credit for them.

You may find that none of the options matches your answer. If so, you should re-read the question, eliminate any obviously wrong answers and select whichever of the remaining options is the most likely to be correct. If you are still unsure, continue to the next question.

Finish off

Revisit unanswered questions. When you come back to a question you will often be able to answer it straightaway. If you are still unsure and are not penalised for incorrect answers, guess - never leave a question unanswered! Make sure also that you have recorded your answers clearly in the way prescribed in the question paper; that you have filled in the answer sheet if you've been given one, or that the marker can see your answer if there's no answer sheet.

Timing

It is easy to run into time trouble if you are doing MCQs. The problem is that some MCQs can be answered instantly; others require working out. However by the end of your allotted time you should have an idea of whether you are near the answer to the MCQ or not. If you think you're nowhere near, leave the question. Note the question number against your rough workings and come back to it later, or just guess.

Wording

There are often many different MCQs that could be asked about the same piece of knowledge. The wording of some MCQs is therefore not straightforward. Not is often a key word in MCQs, as illustrated in the example below.

Example of "verbal gymnastics" which can occur in an MCQ

The correct answer is B. The question is asking which of the statements is not false ie which of the statements is true.

A is false as Dickens was an English novelist, C is false as the Beatles did not come from New York. D is false as not all of the countries listed are in South America; Tunisia is in Africa. (If you answered D, thinking Tunisia was in South America, consider that the question asked for one answer; and 'two plus two is not five' is undoubtedly true.)

Other objective test questions (OTs)

Focus on the requirements

As with MCQs, you might wish firstly to look through all the OTs if you are taking a paper-based exam. This will help you see which questions are easy, and which seem harder or will take time to work out. You may on the other hand prefer to start at the front.

Because there are various types of OTs, you must ensure that you understand what the instructions say about the format of your answer. Markers will be trying to mark most OTs quickly; if your answer is ambiguous, it will be marked wrong. You need to identify whether you have to state an answer in words, or indicate it by ringing or deleting a word.

You must also establish the limits placed on your answer. You may be asked to identify a single word, point, or a phrase. Definition questions may set a word limit that you cannot exceed.

Analyse the details

You may find that you recognise wording in a question when you sit the exam. If the question seems familiar read the requirement carefully - do not assume that it is identical, as the examiner may have inserted traps.

Fill in the blanks

Important elements in question requirements

................, ..., and ....

122

Plan your answer

Some OTs can be answered instantly. However some will take time to answer, involving workings or careful consideration of what precisely you should write. You need to decide the timing of each question, bearing in mind the total time available and the mark allocation.

Write your answer

The key aspect of presentation is making the marker's life easier by avoiding alterations to your answer if possible. Therefore take care when writing the answer down.

> Because of the need for precision, and the difficulty of changing answers once written, you should consider doing some questions in rough first, for example word-limited definitions or diagrams.

If you are stuck at the end of the time that you have allocated to the question, you must move on to the next question.

Finish off

You should check to see that the answers you give are clear, workings are not confused with answers, and that workings are clear if you can get some marks for workings (true for some, but not all, OTs).

For word limit questions, count the words to make sure you have stayed within the limits set. It may be possible to lose a couple of little words if you are a word or two over.

OT examples

CIMA has published the following list of possibles in addition to MCQs.

▶ *Filling in blanks in sentences*

▶ *Ranking items*

▶ *Stating a definition*

▶ *Identifying a key issue, term or figure*

▶ *Completing gaps in a set of data*

▶ *Identifying points/areas on graphs/diagrams*

▶ *Matching items*

▶ *True/false questions*

▶ *Writing brief explanations*

Examples of OTs in addition to MCQs are shown on the next two pages.

Important elements in question requirements

Instructions, Purpose and Scope

Objective test questions - some examples

1   Complete the following graph to depict a semi-variable cost.

£
Total
cost

Level of activity

2   An example of a semi-variable cost is

(Your answer must not exceed 10 words)

3   Fill in the gaps.

In a civil action the   sues the   . The burden of proof is

                              .

4   Is the following statement true or false?

The magistrates' courts deal only with criminal cases.   *TRUE/FALSE*

5   Which court or courts will normally deal with the following cases?

A claim for contractual damages of £21,000

A claim for tortious damages of £51,000

6   Sylvia pays no tax on the first £3,500 of her earnings and then

22%   24%

23%   25%

tax on the remainder of her earnings. She wishes to have gross earnings of £18,435 and wishes to have £15,000 net of tax earnings.

7. A mail order company has kept records of the value of orders received over a period. These are given in the following table.

Value of orders £	Number of orders
5 and under 15	36
15 and under 20	48
20 and under 25	53
25 and under 30	84
30 and under 35	126
35 and under 40	171
40 and under 45	155
45 and under 50	112
50 and under 55	70
55 and under 65	60
65 and under 85	54
	969

Class interval (value of orders) £	Frequency of orders	Height of block
£ 5 < 15	36	A
£ 15 < 20	48	B
£ 20 < 25	53	C
£ 25 < 30	84	D
£ 30 < 35	126	E
£ 35 < 40	171	F
£ 40 < 45	155	G
£ 45 < 50	112	H
£ 50 < 55	70	I
£ 55 < 65	60	J
£ 65 < 85	54	K

Complete the table above by filling in the appropriate numerical value in the space indicated by the letters.

8. Fill in the gaps in the following sentence (one word for each gap).

Banks must _____ in order to make profits but part of their assets must be kept _____ if they are to meet depositors' requirements for withdrawals of _____ .

Essays

Examples

▶ **Stating in detail**

▶ **Defining terms**

▶ **Describing key features**

▶ **Listing items**

▶ **Explaining the meaning**

▶ **Illustrating by example**

Focus on the requirements

The instructions will determine the structure and depth of your essay.

Instructions such as 'list' indicate questions that are primarily tests of knowledge. Instructions such as 'explain' mean the questions are examining understanding as well. Questions testing understanding will require more consideration of underlying concepts and greater description than questions just testing knowledge.

Potentially the biggest pitfall with many essay questions is failure to understand their scope - remember they are testing your ability to select information. Examiners' reports often complain that answers consist of all candidates know about a topic area, and fail to focus on the specific aspects that the question is covering.

Analyse the details

If you are given extra details in the question, these will influence the content of your answer. If you have to describe key features, these will be features significant to the situation given in the question. If you are asked to illustrate by example, you will first look to use the information from the question.

"Describe the most important features of good accounts."

Why might you have problems answering that question as it stands?

Plan your answer

Most essays will need an introduction, main body, and conclusion, and should contain points that are clear and well-linked.

The criteria that you use to check whether your answer plan is complete will vary for each subject.

In a law question, for example, you might ask whether your answer has covered all relevant types of law.

Check also:

▶ Every paragraph will contribute to answering the question
▶ No paragraph will be too long
▶ The answer will be in a logical order

Write your answer

If your answer has to cover a lot of points, you should keep reminding yourself to be careful of timing, and not to spend too long on each point.

The topic of each paragraph should be clearly visible. You can achieve this by giving each paragraph a header, and also by expressing the paragraph's main idea in the first sentence.

Try to avoid long sentences (more than 20 words) and long paragraphs (more than four or five sentences).

Bullet points, without explanation, are usually not enough.

Finish off

Your answer should contain a conclusion. This can refer back to the question or definition that started your answer, or it can highlight the most important points. However simply listing briefly the points you have already made in detail is unlikely to gain you any marks.

You are not told whether the question comes from a financial or management accounting paper, and your answer will depend on whether the accounts are to be used by the company's members and other stakeholders, or as internal management information.

Discussion

Discussion questions test your ability to think critically. Sometimes you will be given a framework for your discussion. On other occasions you will have to choose how best to structure your answer.

Types of discussion

▶ **Compare two subjects**
▶ **Discuss pros and cons**
▶ **Discuss for/against**
▶ **Discuss a proposition**

Propositions

Examples of propositions are whether X causes Y, how X impacts on Y, whether X is classified correctly.

Focus on the requirements

You should consider carefully the scope of your answer.

▶ The aspects of a subject area under discussion – unless you are told to the contrary, each key aspect will need equal treatment
▶ The opinions expressed in the question
▶ The words you will have to define or explain (for example if writing about benefits, why are they benefits)

The instructions may ask you to discuss, or may ask whether you agree with, a proposition. In both instances you will have to show why arguments that are contrary to your viewpoint are not convincing enough. Remember that the issues involved will often not be clearcut.

Analyse the details

The details in the question may indicate the various viewpoints you should consider. If you are not told, think about the various parties who might be involved in the discussion, and who might be interested recipients of your answer.

Interested parties may include management, shareholders, debtholders or the government.

Remember also that you will need to approach the discussion from the perspective of the paper you are sitting. A discussion on an auditing paper would concentrate on implications for audits and auditors, a discussion on a financial accounting paper on the impact on accounts.

"Multiple choice questions are the best means of examining knowledge for lower level papers. Discuss "

Should your answer just cover multiple choice questions?

Plan your answer

Your answer should be structured around clear points, with the interrelationship between them highlighted. Your viewpoint will also influence your structure. You should therefore decide when planning your answer what your conclusion will be. Don't forget however to give due weight to views contrary to your intended conclusion.

An introductory paragraph may help set the discussion in context. However the detailed technical material you use in the body of your discussion needs to be selected carefully to support the points you are making.

> A common shortcoming in answers is excessive technical detail but little development of discussion.

You should check your plan before you start writing to confirm that you have covered all sides of the key issues fairly. Example plans for a discussion question are shown overleaf.

Write your answer

You need to be very careful when writing your answer with your timing, and avoid taking too long over single points or over one part.

Finishing off

You should draw a conclusion based on the previous paragraphs; you should not introduce new material that strengthens your argument. The conclusion should also indicate the key issues (the most significant arguments in favour of a proposition, or the most important differences between X and Y).

Although this proposition is about **multiple choice questions**, and your answer should concentrate on them, it also says that they are the **best** (not a good) way of examining knowledge. You therefore need to discuss whether any other methods might be better.

'It's a waste of time starting to study until a fortnight before the exam. Anything you learn before then you'll have forgotten by the time you come to take the exam.'

Do you agree?

Answer plan 1

Introduction

- ▶ Need to study for longer
- ▶ Can make study prior to previous fortnight effective

Is fortnight before long enough?

- ▶ Focus on essential knowledge/essential techniques
- ▶ Few do pass exams this way

But

- ▶ Syllabuses too large to be covered in fortnight
- ▶ Not enough time for effective question practice?
- ▶ Not time to get help
- ▶ Knowledge crammed in may not be remembered in exam

Study prior to fortnight

- ▶ Possible to remember for longer than fortnight
- ▶ Need to ensure regular recapping
- ▶ Use fortnight before for revision - practice key questions/reminder essential facts

Conclusion

Disagree - not long enough and can study effectively prior to fortnight

Answer plan 2

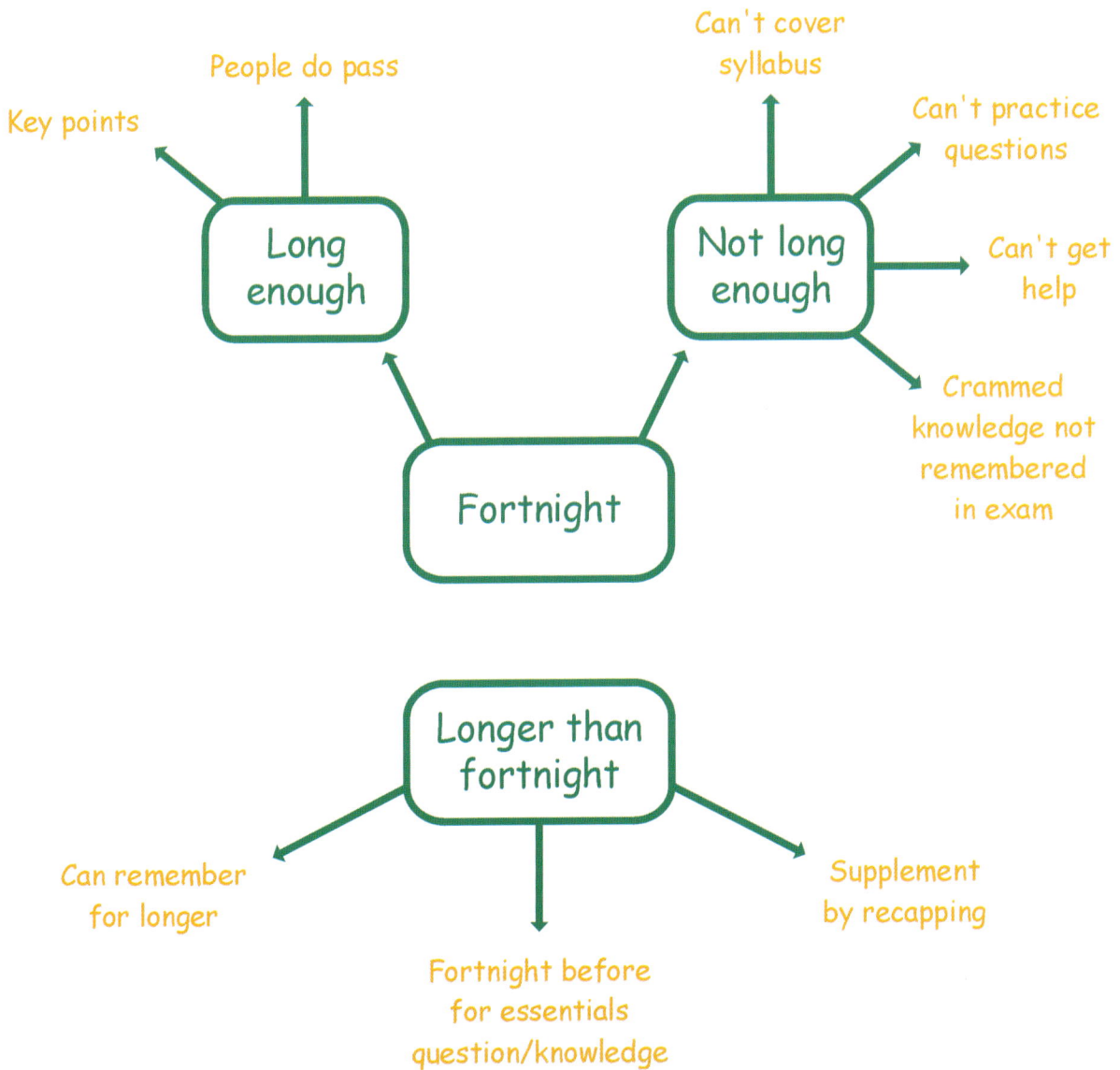

Law problems

Focus on the requirements

The instructions may limit the scope of your answer to a certain area of law, for example consideration of civil (but not criminal) liability, or focusing on certain types of remedy.

If the purpose of your answer is to provide advice to a specific person, your answer should be written from the recipient's perspective, and should only include the issues that affect that person. If you are asked for a general analysis of the situation, you should cover all the main issues, even if certain issues do not affect everyone involved in the situation.

Analyse the details

The situation may well involve more than one legal issue, so make sure you read all the narrative thoroughly.

> The legal issues at stake will vary according to the area of law under discussion. In a criminal law problem, for example, you will be looking for the details that help you determine what crimes have been committed, and what the defences might be.

The legal issues to which you need to pay most attention are ones where there is uncertainty. There may be other points of law involved, but these may be unambiguous, and would warrant only a brief mention in your answer.

As you read through the question, you may identify that the circumstances of the case are similar to a case you have studied. You should note this down but be careful - the examiner might have introduced additional complications.

What should you do if you know that a
legal principle was established in a certain case,
but cannot think of the case name?

Plan your answer

There is a good general model for the structure of answers.

► Identify the legal issues involved in the scenario
► Explain the law
► Apply the law to the facts of the problem
► Conclude, supported by the rest of the answer

You should apply this framework differently depending on the area of law covered in the question. For example, in a contract law question you would discuss who can sue and be sued, on what grounds and with what consequences.

Remember that as well as explaining the law, it may be as important to state the limitations or exceptions to it.

Write your answer

You should concentrate on the principles expressed in relevant cases rather than the facts, and deal briefly, if at all, with issues of minor significance. You can improve the presentation of your answer by underlining statute references and case names.

Finish off

Don't forget the last part of the answer; you must draw a conclusion that is supported by what you have previously said. Don't let fear of reaching a wrong verdict prevent you from drawing a conclusion; remember that you can rarely be certain what the decision will be.

Pitfalls in law exams

"It is not enough for a candidate to conclude that the characters involved in the hypothetical dispute would be held guilty or not guilty without supporting argument. If it (were enough) candidates would have in effect a 50% chance of achieving a pass by guessing."

The quote is taken from an article by a law examiner. The article went on to list regular failings in law exams:

► *Quoting cases and section numbers, but not providing any explanation.*

► *Writing a long list of rules hoping that one will be relevant.*

If you can't think of a case name, don't worry too much. You will normally get credit for stating that the legal principle comes from a decided case, or identifying the case by highlighting its key details in a sentence.

Numerical

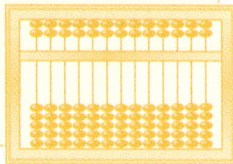

Focus on the requirements

Even for simpler questions, you must follow instructions about what you are supposed to be calculating and what the scope of your answer should be (for example how many months should your cash budget cover?).

If the question does not specify what you should do, think about the purposes of your answer; what will your calculations show, and how will they be used by the recipient. The question details may give more information.

Analyse the details

Drawing a diagram may clarify question details, for example trying to illustrate the group structure in a financial accounting question.

You should look out for figures that are likely to need adjustment. If the information indicates that a figure should be adjusted, mark the figure on the question paper to indicate the adjustment that will be required. In a cash forecast for example, you may need to adjust sales for credit sales and cash received from previous periods' sales.

You should also try to identify irrelevant information or traps, for example details about non-cash items when you are asked to calculate cash movements.

Don't forget to look out for details that will help you answer the written parts of the question.

Give six examples of mathematical techniques other than addition, subtraction, multiplication and division that you will have to use regularly in accountancy exams.

Plan your answer

Think carefully about what calculations you should do.

   ▶   Can you use shortcuts to avoid some of them?
   ▶   Can you do the easier calculations first?
   ▶   Which calculations are the most important?

You may be able to use a step-by-step approach to answer some questions. However the requirements may mean that you don't have to carry out all the possible steps.

The layout of your answer is also important. Not leaving enough room may seriously affect answer presentation.

You will need to decide whether you can do the written parts of questions first, or whether you will need to use the data from your calculations. A key element of timing is giving yourself enough time on the written parts, particularly in higher level papers.

Write your answer

You should try to avoid altering your calculations, as a large number of alterations will make your answer difficult to follow. A lot of the marks may be available for workings so make these clear. An example answer with supporting workings is shown on the next two pages.

Finish off

You should try to find time for some basic checks. These include trying to spot simple errors that hopefully can be corrected easily, also that figures in the main answer are cross-referenced to, and agree with, supporting workings.

A general approach

1 Easier marks

Initial simple calculations, writing out the proforma, putting numbers from the question into the proforma

2 Harder marks

More complicated calculations, calculations using the figures from the simple calculations, adjusting figures given in the question

3 Final stages

Doing the final calculations necessary to produce a result, totalling figures

4 Conclusion

Drawing a conclusion, is the balance sheet strong or weak, should the investment be undertaken, how should the currency risk be hedged etc.

We have listed some common examples below. If you are not comfortable with these, you must practice the techniques; a good business mathematics text will help you.

Calculating percentages and ratios

    Rounding

Approximation

    Manipulation of equations

Interest arithmetic, compounding and discounting

Presentation of data in graphs, charts, diagrams

    Calculating the mean and standard deviation

Use of index numbers

    Probabilities and use of the normal distribution

Panda Limited
Cash Budget for April to June

	Working	April £	May £	June £
Receipts				
Sales	1	2,700	34,020	103,680
Total receipts		2,700	34,020	103,680
Payments				
Materials	2		63,600	42,000
Labour	3	19,200	24,000	24,000
Variable costs	4		4,800	6,000
Fixed costs	5		12,000	12,000
New machinery			60,000	60,000
Total payments		19,200	164,400	144,000
Balance b/f		60,000	43,500	(86,880)
Net cash flow		(16,500)	(130,380)	(40,320)
Balance c/f		43,500	(86,880)	(127,200)

Workings

	April £	May £	June £	July £
1 Sales				
April sales (£27,000)	2,700	24,300		
May sales (£97,200)		9,720	87,480	
June sales (£162,000)			16,200	145,800
Total receipts	2,700	34,020	103,680	145,800
2 Materials				
April purchases (£30,000 + (40 x £840))		63,600		
May purchases (50 x £840)			42,000	
June purchases (50 x £840)				42,000
Total material costs		63,600	42,000	42,000
3 Labour				
April wages (40 x £480)	19,200			
May wages (50 x £480)		24,000		
June wages (50 x £480)			24,000	
Total labour costs	19,200	24,000	24,000	
4 Variable costs				
April (40 x £120)		4,800		
May (50 x £120)			6,000	
June (50 x £120)				6,000
Total variable costs		4,800	6,000	6,000

5 Fixed costs

£15,000 less £3,000 depreciation

Financial analysis

Focus on the requirements

You may be told which ratios you should calculate. Alternatively you may be asked to analyse the data to obtain evidence on important issues, such as recent performance or ability to pay debts.

Pay careful attention to what your analysis will need to discuss. Questions where you just have to carry out calculations are rare even in lower level papers.

> A very common complaint in examiners' reports is that analysis of calculations is insufficient or irrelevant.

Analyse the details

Key things to draw out from the information are:

1 **Obvious changes**. Have a general look at the figures first, to highlight the most significant areas.

2 **Appropriate measures.** Comparisons with previous years may not be of great use if there has been major additional investment.

3 **Detailed measures.** Total profits may be less important than profits for each location or per employee.

4 **Reliability of information.** Consider sources of information; are the company's figures reliable? This may require comment in your answer.

5 **Significance of normal levels.** Industry averages may be of little value if there is wide variation around them.

6 **Likely reasons why figures might deviate.** Look for business reasons that follow from the data you are given, not from wild speculation.

What are the main implications of the following figures?

	20X9 £	20X8 £
Inventory	38,000	10,000
Receivables	16,000	14,000
Trade payables	36,000	12,000

Plan your answer

If you are not told what ratios to calculate, you still need to be selective. Remember the purposes of the analysis, and:

- ▶ **Select the appropriate measures.** Firstly think which commonly-used comparisons may be relevant. Then think if there are any further measures that may also be significant.

- ▶ **Calculate a range of ratios.** If you have to choose what ratios to calculate, you should be choosing ratios that give different perspectives on the business. Your answer will lack breadth, for example, if you calculate four profitability ratios, but don't calculate any ratios relating to solvency.

- ▶ **Decide how far your written analysis should go.** As well as commenting on your calculations, you may need to discuss the limitations of what you have done. Limitations might include lack of data, manipulation of data, and significant non-financial factors.

Write your answer

You should make clear how you have carried out the calculations if there is more than one way of doing so, or what you have done is unusual.

You also need to structure your analysis in the most helpful way for the recipient. It may be best to put your commentary in the main answer, cross-referenced to an appendix containing detailed calculations.

Finish off

If the reader needs to take action, you should recommend what should be done, such as a company buying another company. Alternatively you may have to discuss how the business should remedy problems shown by the analysis.

You would concentrate on finding out the reasons why inventory but not receivables has significantly increased (inability to sell inventory perhaps), and whether the increase in trade payables meant that the company had negotiated more favourable terms with its suppliers or had difficulty paying them.

Ratio analysis of inventory + receivables: trade payables shows a figure of 2 in 20X8 and 1.5 in 20X9. This indicates that the assets provide less security than before for the amounts owed.

Reports

Focus on the requirements

You need to note carefully what the instructions say about who the recipient of the report will be and the purpose for which it will be written.

Purposes of reports

► Assisting management
► Permanent record
► Provision of information
► Record of your own views

The recipient and purpose will influence:

► The content, what information is useful
► The form the report takes
► The language the report uses
► The explanations the report contains

A common failing of many reports (not just in accountancy exams) is that they are packed with jargon that the recipient does not understand, and information that the recipient does not need.

Analyse the details

Not all the information you are given in the question will be relevant. You need to concentrate on the information that will most influence your analysis and the recommendations you will be making.

You may need to make certain assumptions when writing your report. The assumptions you make should be realistic and should be stated clearly in the report.

How can you demonstrate quickly to the examiner that your report fulfils the requirements of the question?

Plan your answer

Your report must have a clear, logical structure. It should emphasise the key points and discuss them in depth. You should take care when selecting the points you intend to make; omitting details because they are contrary to your case may mean your report lacks objectivity.

You should also think about the best format for your report. This includes how you are going to use headings and spaces, and whether you need to include appendices.

We list on the right the details that a long formal report could contain. Shorter reports will not need every stage.

> An informal report may only need an introduction, a summary of findings and a conclusion.

Write your answer

When writing the report, you should be using objective and clear language. It may be better to use third person or impersonal language, rather than 'I' 'We'. As presentation is important, try to avoid crossing outs, alterations etc. Also keep an eye on timing, as your answer may be undermined if you have to omit points due to lack of time.

Finish off

Don't forget the recommendations if these are required. You should also check that all the 'signposts' in the report are clear, with points being cross-referenced to appendices.

Formalities

▶ Title
▶ Report writer
▶ Report recipient
▶ Date

Stages of a long report

▶ Contents
▶ Scope/terms of reference
▶ Information used
▶ Findings, in sections with headings
▶ Summary
▶ Recommendations/ conclusions
▶ Appendices

One good way of doing this is to use the question requirements as the heading for your report.

REPORT

To: Wendy Chan, Managing Director

From: Accountant

Subject: Analysis and recommendations regarding the proposed closure of the factory in Port Said and the move to Alexandria

Scenarios

Focus on the requirements

Sometimes reading the question details very quickly will give you a better idea of what the purpose of your answer is likely to be. However you should not start analysing the situation in detail before you know what you will be doing with the data.

The instructions may specify that your answer should be written for specific recipients. Your answer's scope will be influenced by why they want the information and their level of knowledge. The recipients may be implied by the paper and the instructions; for example a report on a client may be for an audit partner, but an audit programme may be for junior members of your audit team.

Analyse the details

You need to spend time familiarising yourself with the organisation described. This will mean, when you plan and write your answer, that you keep it focused on the scenario's subject.

When analysing the situation, you should look out for key factors that will influence your treatment of the problem, or the recommendations you make.

Possible key factors
- ► Size of organisation and hence the resources it has
- ► Factors influencing decisions
- ► Procedures and controls
- ► Weaknesses

There may also be paper-specific means of analysing the situation, for example using the balance sheet objectives as a means of assessing audit implications.

What is wrong with these recommendations for management

1 Choose a profitable segment.

2 Set a quantified objective.

Plan your answer

When you plan your answer, you may well find you have insufficient time to cover all the relevant issues in depth. This is because the timing is deliberately tight, testing your ability to prioritise and concentrate on the important issues.

Remember also that you may be expected to discuss the limitations of the techniques you use, or other factors you should take into account, even if you are not specifically asked to do so in the question.

The distinction between a scenario and a major case study (see page 136) may be relevant to the techniques you employ. For scenarios you may fall into the trap of using techniques that are too elaborate for the data you are given, or the amount of time you have to answer the question.

Write your answer

You should only bring in relevant information from the question, and do so succinctly; you should not be spending time copying out chunks of the question.

The presentation should be clear, in line with instructions and any answer layout preferences that the examiner has. You should not, however, spend excessive time on over-elaborating the appearance of your answer.

Finish off

You will probably have to offer a conclusion and recommendations. You should make sure that these are clear and specific.

1 You should be giving the examiner specific advice on the criteria to be applied and the decision framework. If you have enough data, you should be making a recommendation yourself.

2 The advice is too general; you yourself need to take it (!), and say something like: 'I recommend that we seek to increase profits to £10 million by 2005. I believe this is achievable because customers will like the increase in product quality etc.'

Example scenario

1

ABC is a listed company that designs and installs heavy manufacturing equipment.

2

The head office of ABC is in a Eurozone member state, but about 70% of its sales are exported. ABC has sales offices in all major regions of the world apart from the Middle East. Sales are always invoiced in the currency of the country in which the equipment is being installed.

3

4

5

The actual manufacturing of the equipment is currently outsourced to a supplier based in another Eurozone member state. Manufacture of the equipment normally takes 4-5 months; ABC's customers pay a deposit on order, then pay a further sum upon delivery and a final sum after the equipment is installed.

6

7

The main functions based at ABC's head offices are a small design team, supply which deals with the suppliers and accounting that deals with the production of the management and financial accounts.

8

9

ABC's board is dominated by Edgar Frere who founded the company twenty-five years ago and is the Chairman and Chief Executive of the company. His son Chris Frere is the Finance Director, and his daughter Antonia Frere is the Purchasing Director. The company does not have a Sales Director on the main board as Edgar Frere considers that sales are within his remit as Chief Executive.

10

11

12

ABC also has two non-executive directors who have no managerial responsibilities. One is the wife of Chris Frere and the other is an old friend of Edgar Frere.

This is the sort of scenario you might encounter in a number of different papers; being given plenty of information about an organisation and having to identify relevant details. We've included in this example coloured font and numbered dialogue boxes indicating important points; see if you can identify why these points might be important before turning to the next page.

Edgar exercises control over the sales offices by a combination of phone calls two or three times a week, use of information generated by the enterprise resource planning system, budgets to control expenses and monthly management accounts which are prepared by the central accounting function from information supplied by the sales offices.

ABC is financed by a mix of share and debt capital. There are 10 million shares in issue with a current market price of €7.20. The company financed a considerable expansion of its sales offices overseas a few years ago with a loan of €10 million, which is repayable in two years' time.

ABC's sales revenues last year were €500 million. For the first time in a number of years, profits fell. Sales only increased by 2% year-on-year because of increasing competition, particularly for sales of high-technology machinery. Major costs are staff salaries and travel expenses; ABC pays above the industry average to attract good staff. Earnings after tax were €8 million.

At the last board meeting. Edgar outlined the following options for expanding the company:

- ▶ Acquisition of the manufacturers of the machinery

- ▶ Acquisition of a company specialising in design and installation of high technology machinery

- ▶ Establishment of sales offices in the Middle East which Edgar believes is a major growth market over the next few years.

13

14

15

16

17

18

19

20

21

22

23

24

Analysis of scenario

1 ABC will have to obey the rules of the stock exchange on which it is listed.

2 Therefore sales prices are likely to be high, but sales volumes are likely to be low.

3 World economic conditions will impact significantly upon demand.

4 ABC is vulnerable to its home currency strengthening against overseas currencies.

5 What controls does ABC exercise over its supplier?

6 Will ABC have to pay its supplier before it receives the bulk of monies from customers?

7 Has ABC invested sufficient resources in design?

8 Will a centralised accounting function be sensitive to the information needs of local offices?

9 ABC is dominated by one man – continuity or inflexibility?

10 Is it appropriate that one man holds both these significant roles?

11 Is therefore sufficient attention being given to sales offices? What are the consequences of Edgar Frere being over-burdened?

12 Non-executive directors are meant to exercise independent scrutiny and if necessary stand up to executive directors. Is it likely that these two will?

13 Is this a sophisticated enough system for the needs of ABC?

14 What types of budgets are being prepared? Are they an effective control?

15 What checks are made on the reliability of information sent from local offices?

16 ABC faces financial risk because of being financed by debt capital.

17 Will ABC have sufficient cash available to repay this debt?

18 Is ABC capable of responding?

19 It may be difficult to control these costs - is ABC getting value for money?

20 Because we are given share price and earnings information, we can calculate the price-earnings ratio (an important figure for investors).

21 Why spend money investing in the supplier? Is it a sign that current arrangements are not satisfactory?

22 Acquiring another company may give the impetus ABC needs to compete better, but there may be problems in merging two different company cultures.

23 There may be significant political risks and cultural issues involved in this investment.

24 What evidence does Edgar have of this?

Links between information

You can see that just going through the scenario has generated lots of thoughts and questions. You can obtain further insights (and indications on how your answer might be structured) by linking information.

Financial information is a good example. Will ABC have funds available to invest further given stagnating sales and the need to repay debt in the near future? ABC being listed means that it has to comply with governance codes, but its domination by Edgar Frere suggests it is not doing so. Has the failure to invest in design been the major cause of poor sales or are other factors involved?

Additional information

Analysis of the scenario not only raises questions about the information we are given, but should also make us consider what we have not been told. Significant information that we have not been given in this scenario includes:

- Whether ABC has shareholders who aren't actively involved in the company; their interests will need to be considered

- Industry financial data, for example typical gearing levels and price-earnings ratios

- Edgar Frere's age; he has been involved with ABC a long time; is he due to retire soon?

- Whether the success of the sales offices is measured using any non-financial measures, such as quality or customer satisfaction indicators

- Whether budgets are being used effectively given the high cost levels

What we have not been told may require comment in our answer, when discussing limitations of our analysis or as a potential weakness of the business (if it's not mentioned, the business may not have it when it should.)

Format of questions

What you are asked to do will depend on the nature of the paper you are sitting. In a management strategy paper you will be focusing on strategy generation and organisation issues; in a risk management paper you will be concentrating on the key risks you've identified. You would be given more numbers in a financial strategy paper to be able to assess the different investment possibilities.

Whatever the paper, this scenario is typical of many you'll see. A company with evident problems and weaknesses, facing the possibility of change and having to consider its consequences. You will have to explain to the board what the problems are, advise them on how to overcome the problems and recommend how to cope with change.

Case studies

Focus on the requirements

You may find it helpful to skim-read the information in the case study before considering the requirements. Do not, however, start analysing the situation before you understand all aspects of the requirements.

1 **Instruction** - generally to make recommendations for decisions

2 **Purpose** - consider the needs of the recipient, and how you in your role can help

3 **Scope** - determined by the decisions, the factors influencing decisions and the context (the business's internal and external, present and future situations)

Analyse the details

As you go through the data, you need to note or highlight clearly the information of great importance. This will be issues that will have most impact on your recommendations, giving perspectives into the company's position, opportunities and challenges and possible courses of action.

You should also think about how you can manipulate the data to gain further insights, by using analysis techniques such as relevant ratio calculations, or what theories you might draw on in your answer.

For case studies involving pre-seen material, the material you are given on the day will have a major impact on your answer. In particular, extra financial data will be highly relevant. You may therefore have to **modify significantly** your previous view of the organisation.

Recommendations

Having seen examples of poor recommendations on a previous page, what are the features of good recommendations?

▶ Clearly justified and prioritised
▶ Follow from previous discussion
▶ Available and viable

▶ Commercially sensible
▶ Within a defined timescale
▶ Specify important impacts

Plan your answer

If the requirement falls into **logical parts**, structure your answer round these. If the requirement is vague, the structure will probably depend on how you've **prioritised** the issues. You must write in most depth about the most significant issues, those that have the **greatest strategic impact**, affect **key stakeholders**, must be **dealt with immediately** or impact upon **survival prospects**.

You should also consider what business models and financial techniques you should use to analyse the material; any analysis done on preseen material will have to be updated. Before you start writing confirm that what you plan to say is **consistent** with preseen and unseen data.

Write your answer

You should start each section on a **separate piece** of paper or a separate page if you're answering on computer. Each section and paragraph should be numbered in a hierarchy.

Appendices should include everything that the user does not need to know immediately. You can also save yourself time by doing your calculations neatly, and putting them in an appendix.

Keep thinking when you're writing 'Will it be clear to the reader why I'm giving this point this degree of attention?'

Finish off

Your **conclusions** and **recommendations** (they are **not** the same!) should be in a **separate section**, backed by the arguments in your report. To ensure that your **conclusions** are supported by evidence, refer in them to the relevant paragraph numbers in your report.

There must be recommendations for all the major issues that have arisen in the unseen. Each recommendation should be around three to four sentences long. A really big issue will have more than one recommendation. You must allow yourself enough time at the end of the exam to produce enough high-quality recommendations - half an hour or more.

“This exam will be about everything and anything you know and are.”

Alan Bennett, *The History Boys*

Case study matrix

Most case studies are marked using a matrix that judges the answer according to a number of different criteria. The example matrix below is based on the marking guides used by the Chartered Institute of Management Accountants and the Institute of Chartered Accountants in England and Wales.

Possible criteria	Possible marks	Main elements
Technical knowledge	5	The knowledge used should be relevant and correct.
Application	10	Knowledge is applied clearly in an analytical and practical manner.
Diversity of detail	10	The answer should include all the key issues and significant viewpoints. Assumptions should be criticised and limitations of data identified as appropriate.
Focus	10	The answer only includes relevant information. The level of detail should be appropriate and key arguments should be developed in depth.
Priorities	10	Most attention should be given to the most important points.
Judgement	15	Judgements are made professionally, with clear recognition of possible solutions.
Integration	10	Different areas of knowledge and skill are combined effectively.
Communication and recommendations	20	The answer should be in a professional style with the necessary degree of formality. The main points should be expressed clearly. The answer should meet the audience's needs. Conclusions and recommendations should be valid and based on the content of the main report.
Ethics	10	The answer evaluates ethical issues well, and provides clear and reasonable advice on them.
	100	

Learning
styles

Types of
subject

Study
environment

Study
skills

Revision

Types of
question

Exam
paper

An
assortment

Exam paper

EXAM PAPER

ANY LEVEL

Any subject

ANY

INSTRUCTIONS TO CANDIDATES

You are allowed as long as you like to read the material in this chapter, and you should refer back to it before taking any accountancy exams.

Complete the checklists on the left-hand pages if you find them helpful. Answer all the quick quiz questions on the right-hand pages. Answers are at the end of the chapter.

Equipment requirements

	Night before	Day of exam
	☐	☐
Pens	☐	☐
Pencils	☐	☐
Pencil sharpener	☐	☐
Rubber	☐	☐
Ruler	☐	☐
Geometrical instruments	☐	☐
Charting template	☐	☐
Calculator(s)	☐	☐
Spare batteries for calculators	☐	☐
Exam entrance documentation including candidate no.	☐	☐
Evidence of identity	☐	☐
Directions to exam centre	☐	☐
Watch	☐	☐
Handkerchief	☐	☐
Medication (hay fever, cough sweets etc)	☐	☐

The day before

Is last minute revision a good idea?

The most you should do is additional light revision of key points. Remind yourself of where you've made mistakes, so that you won't do the same in the exam. Revising topics for the first time just before the exam can crowd out the topics you have revised previously.

You also must try to rest. A good night's sleep the night before will do you far more good than last-minute, late night revision. It really does refresh the brain.

Equipment requirements

We list opposite items that you will need for most exams.

> You may need additional items for certain exams; do not forget to include these in your checklist.

If you can't sleep

If you think that you won't sleep the night before the exam, answer the quick quiz question below. If relaxation techniques don't work, you should nevertheless get into a resting position and make yourself comfortable.

Also don't worry. Doing the exam will provide you with the adrenalin you need to overcome any feelings of physical tiredness. Thinking to yourself that it will not matter if you can't sleep will actually relax you and help you nod off.

> Don't forget to set your alarm. It may be worth buying a second alarm clock, or an alarm clock that will not switch itself off.

Calculators

As well as taking spare batteries and/or a spare calculator, put new batteries in your main calculator and make sure it's working.

If you have a solar-powered calculator, remember that some exam halls are fairly dark, and your calculator may not work well under artificial light. You should consider taking a spare battery-powered calculator.

You should check the exam instructions you have received for details about the types of calculator that are, and are not, acceptable.

Quick quiz 1

Give three examples of relaxation exercises.

Travel arrangements

General

How much time will the journey take?

How much extra time will you allow yourself in case of any hold-ups?

Car

Are there any delays that you can find out about in advance?

Does your car have sufficient petrol, oil etc?

Do you know all details of the route? (The map that accompanies the exam instructions may only show the approach to the exam hall.)

What alternative routes can you use if roads are shut or traffic is too heavy?

Are there garages on your route that you could call into in an emergency?

Are you guaranteed a car parking space?

What will you do if your chosen car park is full?

Public transport (Train/Tram/Bus/Underground)

Have you used an up-to-date copy of the timetable to check running times?

Are there any delays that you can find out about in advance?

Do you know where you have to catch your transport?

Will you have to change transport during the journey?

How long have you allowed to make the connection?

For how long will you be delayed if you fail to make the connection?

Is there an alternative route you can use if there are delays/cancellations on your planned route?

Walk

What do you intend to do if the weather conditions are adverse (being soaking wet is not the best condition to take an exam)?

The day of the exam

What to eat

If you do normally eat breakfast you should certainly have a normal-sized, but not excessive, breakfast. If you don't normally eat first thing, consider nevertheless having something before the exam as it will increase your energy levels.

It's best to avoid drinking excessive amounts of any liquid; you will not earn any marks during toilet breaks!

Directions

You should make sure in advance that you know the way to the exam hall. A practice journey shortly before the exam may help.

You must allow plenty of time to get to the exam hall. One possible rule is aim to arrive at the latest thirty minutes before the exam starts. You might allow more time if your journey is long.

You should consult the radio or television travel news first thing in the morning, and just before you go, to check if there are any delays. These may mean that you have to use an alternative route.

Once there

The only thing you should say about the exam to the other candidates is to wish them luck. You're better off discussing the state of the world, or how you plan to celebrate when the exams are over, than increasing each others' nerves. You may be better off finding somewhere away from other students while you're waiting.

If possible your practice journey should be at similar times to your actual journey. Travel conditions and timetables at the weekend may be very different to those you experience in the rush hour on the day of the exam.

Quick quiz 2

What can you do if you do arrive late for the exam?

Initial stages

Personal details

✓ Fill in your candidate number, centre details and other details on the front of your answer booklet.

Timing

✓ Check your watch with the clock in the exam room.

✓ Check how long you have to answer the paper, and write down the finishing time.

Format of paper

✓ Identify which questions are compulsory.

✓ Check whether you have to answer a certain number of questions from certain sections of the paper.

✓ Confirm how many optional questions you have to do.

✓ Ascertain the number of marks available for each question.

Reading through the exam paper

✓ Rank the optional questions based on the requirements of the **whole** question.

✓ Confirm that you are happy with the optional questions you have chosen.

✓ Write down the list of questions you intend to do and the order you intend to answer them.

✓ Confirm that your list includes **all** the compulsory questions and the **correct number** of **optional** questions.

✓ Allocate time to the questions in accordance with the number of marks available for each question, and allowing for time spent reading the paper and checking your answers at the end.

You will be sitting in the exam room for the next few hours. You won't achieve anything if you do nothing; you will achieve something if you pick up your pen and start writing.

The start of the exam

Initial reactions

You may think that the paper is nowhere near as bad as you expected. You can answer all the questions and the only issue is how much you can write in the time available.

> Be careful! Adrenalin can be a very positive stimulus, but it can lead to excessive speed. If you rush at the start of the exam, you may choose the wrong questions or misunderstand what is being asked.

However you may feel that the paper is much harder than you ever thought it could be.

> But lots of others will be feeling the same! Everyone will have to do that difficult-looking compulsory question. You don't have to do that impossible optional question.

One way to limit the impact of your reactions is to spend the first few moments checking the timing and format of the paper. Completing these tasks will calm you down and settle you into the exam.

Reading through the paper

You must decide which questions to do, and the order in which you will do them. You may want to read through the paper twice to make the right choices.

As you are reading, you will find it useful to underline the key words in the question and jot down the most important points. This will help you decide which questions to do, and also aid your memory when you come to answer each question.

Some accountancy bodies allow students reading time in addition to the three hours of the exam. If you are taking an exam with reading time, you must have a plan on how to approach it; you shouldn't spend it generally flicking through the exam paper. Possible uses include:

▶ *Analysing the longest question on the paper*

▶ *Choosing which optional questions to do*

▶ *Seeing how many objective test questions you can answer*

Quick quiz 3

What should you do . . .

(a)   If a hot tip topic that you have revised thoroughly fails to appear on the paper?

(b)   You are set a wholly written question on a topic that has previously only been examined by numerical questions?

Choosing questions

Criteria to use

Topics

How comfortable you feel with the areas covered by the question will be a key influence on whether you choose it; but see below.

Requirements

The requirements for some questions may be less onerous than others, requiring for example less depth of discussion. Whether requirements are broken down into parts or not may make the question easier to understand.

Scenario

Consider how easy it will be to apply the requirements to the scenario you are given.

Easy marks

It may be possible to gain a significant number of marks quickly before you tackle the difficult parts of the question.

Watch out for

Topics

The question may be asking about an aspect of the topic you are less familiar with, or require greater depth of explanation than you have been expecting.

Topics (again!)

The question may not just cover your favourite topics, but also include other topics that you like far less.

Requirements

Beware of answering questions containing requirements that you are not sure you understand.

Unfamiliar terms

Again be careful, but don't let unfamiliar terminology put you off doing the question if you are **sure** you know what it is asking.

Mass of detail

Some questions will give a lot more detail than others. However it may be easy enough to work through the detail provided you adopt a logical approach. Indeed the main challenge in the question may be separating relevant detail from irrelevant, and once you have done that, the question will be straightforward.

Question selection

Choosing questions

You should read the questions carefully to ensure that you are choosing the best optional questions. We list opposite criteria you can use, and also indicate what can lead you to make the wrong decision.

One way to choose questions is to **grade** each question and choose the questions with the highest grades. Alternatively you can try to work out quickly how many marks you think you can gain on each question.

Order of questions

You should also decide at the start of the exam the order in which you will tackle the questions. There are strong arguments for doing the question you think is easiest first. Starting with your best question will ease you into the exam and also increase your confidence when you attempt the more difficult questions later on.

If the exam has MCQs or short answer questions, it is often best to do these first as you'll always be able to answer some of them, and no question will be that complex.

When you come to do certain questions, you may want to tackle the easier parts of the question first. If you answer a multi-part question out of sequence, check that the answers to the parts you answer first do not depend on the answers to the other parts. Also make sure that the marker can see clearly what you've done. Be warned however that many examiners dislike questions being answered out of sequence.

Before you start answering questions, it is worth having one further look through the optional questions, to confirm you are making the right choice.

1	Q5	9.50
2	Q6	10.30
3	Q2	11.10
4	Q1	11.50

Quick quiz 4

If the exam has a large compulsory question, for many more marks than any of the other questions, when should you attempt that question?

Doing questions

Focus on the requirements
- ✓ Skills and depth of understanding
- ✓ Purpose of answer
- ✓ Breadth of answer
- ✓ Marks available for each part of question

Analyse the details
- ✓ Key information
- ✓ Irrelevant material
- ✓ Traps
- ✓ Availability of easy marks
- ✓ Hints from the question on answer structure
- ✓ Overlap between areas covered by different parts of question

Plan your answer
- ✓ All necessary points included
- ✓ Points covered in sufficient detail
- ✓ Irrelevant material excluded
- ✓ Clear order and structure of answer
- ✓ Time allocated for answer reflects available marks

Write your answer
- ✓ Each point made contributes to answering question set
- ✓ Question number/part identified
- ✓ Handwriting and calculations clear
- ✓ Correct layout/format
- ✓ Paragraphs headed
- ✓ Paragraphs and sentences not too long
- ✓ Paragraphs well-structured
- ✓ Language appropriate (formality and technical content)
- ✓ No over-run on question timing

Finish off
- ✓ Calculations totalled
- ✓ Recommendations made and conclusions drawn
- ✓ Answer linked to workings/appendices

Check your answer (see later in this chapter)

Reading and planning

Adopting a disciplined approach

Be warned; you can lose a lot of marks if you rush in and forget what you've learnt about approaching questions.

Reading the question

Certain questions may strike you as familiar when you read the question paper. However it is very dangerous to assume that a question is identical. Answers may have been jumbled up on an otherwise identical MCQ. More complicated scenarios that seem on first glance to be the same will have different complications. To avoid misinterpreting questions, you should read them thoroughly, and read them twice.

Planning your answers

You may find it helpful at the start of the exam to jot down the points we made about planning at the start of Chapter 6, to remind yourself of what you should do when planning your answer.

Don't be put off by seeing people starting to scribble answers down straightaway. They will be throwing marks away by producing answers that are unfocused, unstructured and irrelevant.

Keep reminding yourself

You should remind yourself constantly, whilst answering questions, of the needs to present your answer well, to stay focused on the requirements of the question.

Be selective

Remember when you're planning that being selective is very often the key to producing a firmly focused answer.

You won't get marks for producing paragraphs that don't contribute to answering the question, or evidence that doesn't support the points you're making.

Quick quiz 5

Give two examples of verbs you might find in question requirements that test:

(a)   Knowledge and understanding
(b)   Application of knowledge
(c)   Analysis and evaluation skills

An anti-checklist

Some students, if they are struggling with questions, try a number of strategies designed to confuse markers or enlist their sympathy. If you are tempted to try any of the list below, don't.

Markers are well aware of what students might attempt, and some of the tricks below may even cost you marks. For example, by writing down everything you know about a broad topic area, relevant or irrelevant, you may leave yourself insufficient time to develop the points that are relevant in sufficient detail. Examiner's prefer shorter, focussed answers to longer waffly ones, and may see your inability to concentrate on what they ask for as a sign you lack the skills required to pass that exam.

What not to do

✗ Write over-lengthy introductions and conclusions whilst failing to develop the main body of your answer

✗ Provide uncalled for features such as situation analyses, executive summaries, background information

✗ Make endless assumptions or assumptions that transform what you have been asked to do into a different question

✗ Write what you want to say rather than what the examiner wants you to say

✗ Waffle!

✗ Write illegibly

✗ Provide an unclear structure hoping that the marker will get confused and give you the benefit of the doubt

✗ Use lots of technical jargon, write down whatever technical rules occur to you

✗ Pad out your answer by merely repeating the information given in the question and not using it to support your answer

✗ Tell the examiner what a hard life you've had and don't forget the good wishes for holidays etc.

Dealing with difficulties

Problems with questions

If the question appears difficult when you start answering it, jot down some ideas. Then ask what you need to do to fill in the gaps in your plan.

You may need to make assumptions to answer the question; your ability to come up with reasonable assumptions may be being tested. Your assumptions should be clearly stated at the start of your answer. However you must confirm before you begin writing your answer that your assumptions are reasonable and necessary.

> Read the question again to see whether there is information you missed on earlier readings which means that your assumptions are unnecessary. Also check that your assumptions are needed to answer the question.

Panic

If you find yourself getting stressed, pause briefly. Read the requirements again to confirm you are on the right track. If you are struggling with part of a calculation, remember what you are struggling with is only worth a few marks. Panic is normally not rational, just a manifestation of nerves.

Going back to questions

If you run out of time on a question, or feel you are stuck for now but might be able to say more if you come back to it later, leave plenty of space in your answer booklet and move on. If you do add extra points later on, make sure the answer's structure remains clear and the conclusion is apparent.

The assumptions you make may be a way of twisting the question away from what it actually asks, and towards what you would like it to ask.

Quick quiz 6

Why might the examiner be testing your ability to make assumptions?

Checking your paper

Exam details

✓   All necessary information on front of answer booklet is filled in.

Presentation and clarity

✓   Plan is clearly differentiated from main answer.
✓   Different parts of questions are labelled clearly.
✓   Formal documents (reports, letters etc) are headed correctly.
✓   Headers, underlinings are included if they are helpful.
✓   Final total or conclusion to answer is clearly shown.
✓   Where the answer ends is clear.
✓   Any work that you do not want the examiner to mark is crossed out.
✓   For MCQ papers, answer is clear and there are no other marks that could be read as answers. Also ensure that all MCQs have an answer.

Spelling and grammar

✓   Spelling and grammar are correct.
✓   Meaning of sentences is clear.

Arithmetic

✓   Arithmetic of answers is correct.

Workings

✓   Figures in main answer are cross-referenced to workings.
✓   Figures in main answer agree with workings.
✓   Main answer is clearly differentiated from workings.
✓   Arithmetic of workings is correct.

Appendices

✓   Main answer is appropriately cross-referenced to appendices.
✓   Main answer is clearly differentiated from appendices.

The end of the exam

Last question

When answering the last question, you may find you have one of two problems.

▶ You are struggling to come up with an answer. Rather than getting bogged down on one part, make sure you answer each part of the question.

▶ You are running short of time. The way to make the best use of the time is again to obtain the easy marks first.

For numerical questions this means writing out formats and entering quickly the simplest figures.
For written questions, you should produce a clear plan, make sure your answer has an introduction and conclusion and try to cover your best points.

Checking your work

For most papers it will be worth allocating a few minutes for checks that could gain or save you marks. If your checks identify problems that cannot be rectified in the time available (such as an arithmetic error in the first line of a long calculation question), add a note to your answer. Providing you have used the correct method in your answer, you should gain enough marks to pass the question. Also make sure you've filled in the details on the front of your script correctly.

After the exam

As soon as you leave the exam, you should forget about it and concentrate on the next one, or if it is the last exam, celebrate! Don't discuss the paper with other candidates; there's nothing more you can do on it so why talk about it.

Don't let worrying about the exam affect your life. Lots of successful candidates reach the end of an exam sitting feeling they had at least one bad paper

Quick quiz 7

How can you avoid running short of time on the last question?

Sitting Foundation exams on the computer

Before the exam

Remember that you should have practised taking complete mock exams in the **same format** as your actual exam. Use BPP's i-Pass! This will show you the different types of question, how questions are presented and other features of the software (how it shows you which questions you've done for example). You need to be sure of **what you have to enter** and whether the software can cope with **misspellings**. You need to check before the exam what you will be expected to bring and what the exam body will provide. In particular check whether you will be provided with a calculator and pen.

Going through the exam

Unlike a paper-based exam you won't be able to glance at through all of the exam to see quickly which questions look tough and which questions will take longer to answer. Going through all the questions without entering an answer to any is not a good use of time. We thus recommend that you **attempt the questions one-by-one**, bearing in mind what we say about time management. Make a note of any you weren't sure of, so that you can go back to them.

Keeping to time

Our advice is to **deduct 15 minutes from the total exam time** and **divide this figure by the number of questions** to give you how long on average you should spend on each question. That should leave you a few minutes to revisit doubtful questions. You should be able to answer some questions instantly but others will require more working out. The computer may well indicate the amount of time you have left by a clock on the screen. This is a useful reminder but it is important not to let it panic you.

Dealing with difficulties

If you are unsure about a question, we advise entering what appears to be the **most sensible answer** and coming back to the question in the last 15 minutes at the end of the exam. It's better to enter an answer you're not sure of rather than risk leaving the question unanswered because you run short of time at the end.

Some exam software allows you to specify which questions you'd like to review again so you can access them easily; in other exams you may have to note them down yourself separately. If you've done workings, you should indicate the question to which they relate so that you can review them again as well.

Sitting higher-level exams on the computer

Before the exam

You should practise sitting a complete exam on computer, using **software with the same features** as you will use in the actual exam. In particular you need to be aware whether the software indicates **spelling or grammatical errors**. If you normally use these features to pick up any problems, you will either have to type slower to ensure accuracy or leave time at the end to check spelling and grammar.

Keeping to time

The same considerations apply to a computer-based as to a paper-based exam; you should have planned in advance **how to allocate your time** between different questions. It's important to leave time at the end to go through the exam quickly, correct any errors and improve presentation. However it's possible to spend too much time making the answer look well-presented; a simple, clear document with frequent headings and concise paragraphs will please markers.

Dealing with difficulties

Taking the exam on computer makes it easier to reorganise your answer by **cutting and pasting** if you have second thoughts. Our advice is to be cautious about this; it shouldn't happen if you've thought carefully about your plan. Also think carefully about **workings**. It may take time to set them out clearly, but if you go wrong, the examiner can't give you any credit for workings that aren't there.

If you have any difficulties with the software, you should inform the invigilators immediately.

At present a few higher-level exams, such as CIMA's TOPCIMA exam, can be sat in either computer or paper based formats. Bear in mind what we discussed in Chapter 4 if you can choose the format of your exam.

Over the next few years, accountancy bodies may increase the number of exams that can be sat on computer.

Answers to quick quiz

1
- ▶ Lying on the floor and relaxing your toes
- ▶ Lying in a bath with some relaxing music on
- ▶ Dancing away your frustrations

2 With most exams you should be allowed to take the paper provided you don't arrive too late. You will maximise your chances of passing if you attempt all parts of all questions, but let your time allocation for each part reflect the reduced time that you have available.

If you arrive too late to be allowed to sit the exam, you should still sit the remaining papers after the one you missed. Even if the exam board rule that you must take a group of papers together, they may allow you to take the paper you missed separately next sitting if your lateness was unavoidable.

3
(a) Forget about it! What isn't on the paper has no importance.
(b) Answer the question if it is compulsory; if the question is optional, don't let the fact that it is in an unusual format necessarily put you off answering it. It may still be easier than other optional questions.

If you feel a sense of injustice, bear in mind that the paper will be carefully analysed by tutors and the accountancy press, and the examiner will be made well aware of its shortcomings. Allowances will be made in the marking of problematic papers.

4 Very often the large compulsory question will be the most difficult question on the paper. If you do it first, and struggle, there is a risk that your confidence will be sapped for the rest of the paper.

You should consider doing it first if you feel it is reasonable, to put it behind you. Even if it appears difficult, you should avoid doing it last, and rushing it, as it is the most significant question on the paper.

5 Two examples from:
(a) Define, describe, distinguish, explain, identify, illustrate, list, outline, state, summarise, trace
(b) Apply, calculate, compute, demonstrate, prepare, produce, reconcile, solve, tabulate
(c) Advise, analyse, categorise, compare, consider, contrast, criticise, discuss, evaluate, interpret, justify, recommend, review

6 The assumptions you make may be a good test of your business awareness. For example if you are told that the business just employs the owner and a couple of other employees, you can assume that there will not be the types of elaborate controls that would be necessary in a large company. You can also assume that the finance available to the business will be limited (because of its size and circumstances, the business will not be seeking to raise money through the stock market in the near future, for example).

7
(a) Take the total time available for the examination.
(b) Subtract the time spent reading through the paper to select questions.
(c) Subtract the time allocated at the end for checking the answers.
(d) Take the remaining time and allocate it amongst the questions **according to the marks available for each question**.
(e) When you have decided the order in which you will do the questions, write down against each question the time when you should stop working on the question.
(f) When working on a question, and the time to stop arrives, move on to the next question.

Learning
styles

Types of
subject

Study
environment

Study
skills

Revision

Types of
question

Exam
paper

An
assortment

An assortment

Answer
weaknesses

Presentation
problems

Good
grammar

Coping
with failure

What else
to read

An assortment

Though this section is a collection of items that we have had trouble fitting in elsewhere (and is also designed for those who like lists at ends of books!) the material covered in it is some of the most important in the whole book. We have therefore not called this collection appendices, and thus implied that somehow what's in it is less important.

Most of the lists are based on comments made by examiners in examiners' reports and at examiners' conferences. Examiners' conferences can be rather depressing affairs when you hear law and management accounting, financial management and tax examiners identify exactly the same weaknesses. If you can avoid all the problems and weaknesses we have identified, you will most definitely improve your own chances.

Top Ten answer weaknesses

Weaknesses	Remedies
Giving general answers when specific knowledge or analysis is required	Read the requirements carefully to ensure you understand the scope of the question
Answering in a series of single line bullet points when more depth of discussion is required	Remember what you've been taught during revision about how to construct answers. A good model is to: ▶ Make the point ▶ Explain the point (show why it's important) ▶ Illustrate the point (with scenario material or a real-life example)
Failing to spend enough time on the question with the highest marks	Often this happens when the question is done last and time runs out at the end of the exam. Avoid doing it last and consider doing it first
Failing to answer enough questions	At the start of the exam, note down all the questions you're answering and ensure that your list includes all compulsory questions and enough optional questions. Then allocate time between questions and stick to the time allocation
Not commenting on the results of calculations	You need to comment on what the calculations show and the reasons for the results, also the results' limitations (lack of available data, unrealistic assumptions, need to use additional techniques)
Failing to use the details in the scenario	When analysing the details, mark against them to which part of the answer they relate; refer in your plan to the detail you'll use
Copying out chunks of the scenario which don't add value to the answer	Ask yourself when planning your answer whether the scenario detail you intend to include illustrates the points you intend to make.
Including theories that aren't relevant to the organisation	For each theory you intend to use ask yourself what insights it will give you and only include it if it gives you significant insights
Repeating material in different parts of the same answer	Review your plan before you start writing to ensure there's no overlap between the material used in each part of the question
Reproducing old answers as answers to different questions	Remember that old questions are in the past; what matters is the present and answering this question

To sum this list up: **Not providing what the question requires!**

Top Ten presentation problems

1. Using pencil rather than ink.

2. Using lots of different colour inks.

4. Scattering different parts of the same

5. Failing to show workings or not linking answers clearly to workings.

answer throughout the answer booklet.

6. Unclear handwriting.

7. Failing to fill in the front sheet clearly.

Failing to show clearly what question is being attempted.

8. Not including any headings.   Failing to use basic proformas for example report format or tax computation. 9.

10. Overlong paragraphs

Top Ten rules of grammar

1 Never use a preposition to end a sentence with.

2 Don't use no double negatives.

3 Its important to use apostrophe's correctly.

4 Always re-read your writing to make sure haven't missed any out.

5 Give slang the elbow.

6 The passive voice should never be used.

7 No sentence fragments.

8 Have you used question marks when necessary

9 Don't say things twice, and avoid repeating yourself.

10 Last but not least, avoid clichés like the plague.

How to cope with failing exams

Hopefully these pages won't apply to you.

If they do, we're very sorry.

The most important thing to do is not to get depressed but to come back and pass next time. You can greatly improve your chances by following a clear strategy

1. Understand why you failed

A painful question to answer we know, but one you must address. The page opposite lists the questions you should consider.

As a result of thinking about these questions you may conclude:

▶ You were underprepared for the exam and did not have enough knowledge to attempt it

▶ You were underprepared for the exam and had not developed the necessary skills to answer the questions properly

▶ You approached the exam poorly (question choice, timing etc)

2. Addressing your problems

If you did lack knowledge of certain areas, this time you do need to go back and study them.

However as we've discussed elsewhere, examiners have stated that more students fail because of a lack of application skills or a failure of exam technique. Question practice has therefore to be central to addressing weaknesses in these areas; you can use passcards or Success CDs to revise most areas of the syllabus rather than going back to the text.

Question-based revision courses will help you more than courses where there's more lecturing.

▶ You need to practise questions in full this time, against the clock, without looking at our answer until you've finished yours.

▶ If certain types of question gave you difficulty, do more of them and get help if you're still struggling.

▶ As well as practising individual questions, do complete mock exams against the clock to improve your exam technique.

▶ Find someone else who will mark your answers critically, highlighting weaknesses such as lack of explanation, irrelevant material and poor presentation.

Exam diagnostic

Study

▶ Did you fail to spend enough time on areas of the syllabus when you were studying or revising?

▶ Did you test yourself while you are studying by quick quizzes, i-Pass questions or full questions in the text?

▶ Did you attempt the course exams and submit them on time for marking?

▶ Did the course exams you took highlight any weaknesses and did you address them? Yes we know you probably threw them away immediately after you sat the actual exam, but please try to remember.

Revision

▶ Did you attempt enough questions in full during your revision or did you only practise certain areas?

▶ Did you compare your answers to the model answers critically and work through where you went wrong?

▶ Did you not do any question practice but just re-read your notes and audit the answers in the kit?

▶ Did certain types of question give you difficulties during your revision, and did you seek help on these?

▶ Which questions gave you difficulty on the paper and why?

The exam day

▶ Do you feel you panicked on the day of the exam?

▶ Did you choose the best optional questions?

▶ Did you follow the advice on exam technique you were given, or did you fail to answer enough questions, run short of time at the end or present your work poorly?

Other books you might find helpful . . .

Acres D. (1998) *Passing Exams Without Anxiety.* (5th Ed). Oxford: How to Books Ltd

Good on revision

Buzan T. (1988) *Make the Most of Your Mind.* (2nd Ed). London: Pan Books

Buzan T. (1998) *Master your Memory.* (3rd Ed). London: BBC Worldwide Ltd

This is the book to read for detail on how mindmapping works etc ...

Buzan T. (1995) *The Mind Map Book.* (2nd Ed). London: BBC Worldwide Ltd

Buzan T. (1995) *Use your Head.* (4th Ed). London: BBC Worldwide Ltd

This book is helpful on reading and memory in particular

Chambers E. and Northedge A. (1997) *The Arts Good Study Guide.* (1st Ed). Milton Keynes: The Open University

Coman M. and Heavers K. (1998) *Improve your Study Skills.* (3rd Ed). Chicago: NTC Learningworks

This book is excellent! I would strongly recommend it as general book on study skills

Cottrell S. (1999) *The Study Skills Handbook.* (1st Ed). Hampshire: Macmillan Press Ltd

Drew S. and Bingham R. (1997) *The Student Skills Guide.* (1st Ed). Hampshire: Gower Publishing Ltd

Giles K. and Hedge N. (1995) *The Manager's Good Study Guide.* (2nd Ed). Milton Keynes: The Open University

Kemble B. (1980) *How to Pass Exams.* (1st Ed). London: Orbach & Chambers Ltd

McVea H. and Clumper P. (1996) *Learning Exam Skills.* (1st Ed). London: Blackstone Press Limited

This book deals with law specifically

Northedge A. (1990) *The Good Study Guide.* (1st Ed). Milton Keynes: The Open University

Good on essays

O'Brien D. (1995) *How to Pass Exams.* (1st Ed). London: Headline Book Publishing

Orr F. (1985) *How to Pass Exams.* (1st Ed). London: HarperCollinsPublishers

Lots of bite sized tips to dip into

Race P. (1992) *500 Tips for Students.* (1st Ed). Oxford: Blackwell Publishers Ltd

Rose C. and Goll L. (1992) *Accelerate your Learning.* (1st Ed). Aylesbury: Accelerated Learning Systems Ltd

Svantesson I. (1998) *Learning Maps and Memory Skills.* (2nd Ed). London: Kogan Page Ltd

Another useful look at mindmapping

Williams K. (1989) *Study Skills.* (1st Ed). Hampshire: The Macmillan Press Ltd

This book has a good section on notetaking

And . . .

BPP's courses and study materials are designed help you learn accountancy.